Vimal Vachhani

Jack of All Trades Master of Some

An Introduction to Consulting

www.jackofalltradesmasterofsome.com

Dedicated to all the mentors, managers, educators and bosses that helped provide guidance along the way as well as all the flight agents that ever helped me make a really tight connection.

CONTENTS

Introduction	9
Consulting - A Primer	13
What is Consulting?	13
Why People Hire Consultants. The Math.	14
How Consulting Works	16
Key Metrics	19
Margin and Margin Percentage	19
Utilization	19
Meeting Cost Calculator	21
Project Overrun	21
Fixed Bid Projects vs. Time and Material	21
Independent vs. Firms	22
Compensation, Benefits and Pay Growth Expectations	23
Company Sizes	25
The Big Firm	25
The Small Firm	27
Getting Hired	29
Resumes	31
The Case Study Interview	33
Consulting 101	35
Optics	35

Attire	36
What Does My Client Do?	37
Questions and How to Ask Them	38
I can Teach it to You, but I cannot Understand it for You	40
Quick Wins and How to Say No	42
Scope Creep	44
Scoping the Work Correctly	44
Under Promise, Over Deliver	45
Land and Expand	46
Ethics and Lying	47
The War Room/Consulting Pit	50
Imposter Syndrome	51
Dealing with the age gap	52
Water Cooler Talk	54
Cursing	56
Discussing Race, Religion, Politics, Sexual Orientation	56
Email Etiquette	57
Offshoring	59
Onsite and Offsite Locations	60
Working Remote	60
Never Burn a Bridge and saying Goodbye	61
Consulting Key Phrases	62

50-Thousand-Foot View	62
Low Hanging Fruit	62
Let's Circle Back Around to That	62
Boiling the Ocean	63
Peeling the onion	63
Sticker Shock	63
SOW (Statement of Work)	64
RFP (Request for proposal)	64
Non-Disclosure Agreement (NDA)	64
Master Services Agreement (MSA)	64
Sensitive Data	65
Office Space Etiquette	66
Your Desk	66
Coffee	66
The Microwave and Fridge	68
Travel	70
90% Travel Required	70
Paying the Bills	70
Expense Reports	71
Credit Card Perks	72
Double Hop Travel	73
Travel Efficiency	73

Ride Sharing	77
Dining	77
Staying in Shape	79
Being Kind while Traveling	80
People and Personalities	82
Personalities	82
The Go-Getter	82
The Grouchy IT Guy	82
The Person that should Avoid Buses	83
Chatty Kathy	84
Grinders	85
Unsure New Guy	86
People and Roles	88
Business Analyst	88
Technical Analyst	88
Quality Assurance	89
Sales	89
The Partner	90
Project Manager	91
Project Sponsor/Stakeholders	92
Business Skills	93
Accounting	93

- Operations and Supply Chain ... 94
- Information Technology (IT) ... 95
- Human Resources ... 96
- Management ... 97

Business Skills through the life of a project ... 98
- Roadmap ... 98
- Requirements and Requirement Gathering ... 99
- Development and Delivery Phase ... 102
  - Agile Development vs. Waterfall ... 103
- Environments, Unit Testing and Releasing to Test ... 104
- QA and Testing ... 105
- User Acceptance Testing ... 106
- Go Live and Deployment ... 107
- Support, Documentation and Training ... 108

Disaster Recovery ... 109

Tools Tips and Tricks ... 110
- Spreadsheets ... 110
- Presentations ... 112
- Task Tracking and To Do List ... 114
- Screen Shares, Video Shares and Conference Calls ... 115
- Flow Charts and Process Flows ... 118
- White Boarding ... 119

Programming	120
Focus	120
Interview Questions	122
Tell us about yourself?	122
Why are you interested in consulting?	123
Tell me about a time you displayed leadership?	123
Tell me about a difficult problem you occurred in the past and how you overcame it?	124
Why do you want to work for this firm?	124
What are your strengths and weaknesses?	125
Logical Thinking Questions	125
More Questions	126
Conclusion	128

INTRODUCTION
The First Job

"I hope you don't bomb your first day of work like you bombed your interview".

These were the first words spoken to me by my manager as I started my first real job leaving college. In 2005, as I graduated with a dual degree in Computer Science and Software Engineering. I had landed a job as an application support specialist at a global telecom firm. One week prior, I left the interview—discouraged and disoriented—and stopped at a McDonald's to enjoy a chicken sandwich and small fries to forget the interview I just bombed. That following week, to my surprise, I received a call from the recruiter informing me that I had landed the position. They offered me eighteen dollars an hour to take the role. I was rich! It was the highest paying position I had ever been offered, and it was at one of the biggest companies in the world. In my head, my future at this company played out. I would ascend through the ranks and get a 401K (whatever that was) and would one day make seventy-five thousand dollars a year and live a life of comfort, stability and work satisfaction. I went back to McDonald's that night to celebrate with a buddy and splurged on three items from the dollar menu. I was sitting pretty and about to make some serious cash!

Fast forward 4 months.

I sat in my half-height cubicle, the kind of cubicle that gives you ultimate privacy. The kind of privacy whose only weakness is standing up and tilting your head down more than fifteen degrees. I was tasked with cycling through three years of application support tickets, about 3500 logged incidents at the time, and appending a two-digit acronym to each ticket based on the classification type. Looking around the room at some of the "lifers", I saw little trophies celebrating five, ten, twenty-five-year anniversaries and the modem equivalents of the "hang in there" kitten on the clothesline motivational poster. I decided then and there that if I ever received a twenty-five-year appreciation trophy from this place, I would immediately use it to hit myself over the head repeatedly. I knew working in industry was not the right place for me regarding who I wanted to be and where I wanted to go.

Sorry, that got a little dramatic. In fact, I am grateful for the experience I had and for the folks I got to work with as I first entered the workforce. It allowed me to learn very quickly what I did not want to do, which is just as important as learning what I wanted to do. I've always been the type of personality that thrives on learning new things, having new experiences and being surrounded by experts, pros and other people that function at high velocity. I wanted to work on solving real and complex problems and never just being content with a regular nine-to-five job. Also, being twenty-two at the time, the idea of being able to jet around the country on someone else's dime was cool too. I wanted to be a consultant.

I started applying to every consulting firm I could find. After a month and multiple rejections for lack of experience, I got an offer at a six-person consulting shop focused on pharmaceuticals. When my big-company manager asked me what it would take to keep me, I explained how I felt and what I really wanted to do. He was very understanding and wished me the best. He also could not match my new offer of a staggering forty-five thousand dollars a year. I celebrated with premium non-dollar menu items at Chik-fil-A that night.

Current State

As I sit down to write this book, I am closing in on my fourteenth year of consulting. I have long since abandoned my core C++ and Java programming skills I learned in school and went into a data-driven Business intelligence role, which has allowed me to see the best of all worlds in an organization from the front office, back office and their technical setups. Living in the data has given me a unique view into not only the lifeblood of how an organization really operates, but also a rich history of how it operated in the past and the opportunities it may have in the future.

In my fourteen years, I've been on twenty different projects, working in nine different industries, and I have stayed in hotels in over fifteen different cities. I've eaten in one of the finest restaurants in New York City as well as cardboard pizza from the Greenspoint Houston Mall—lovingly referred to as "Gunspoint" mall by the locals. I have worked in tiny boutique firms as well as large worldwide sized firms. I've had the privilege to work with some of the finest doctors in the country, disgustingly wealthy hedge fund partners, and I have spent hundreds of hours with "Janice from accounting" sifting through spreadsheets, or listening to "Steve from operations" complain about his boss and his two other offers lined up. FYI, Steve is not going anywhere.

Of course, my experience in consulting has had its highs and lows. There are days with fist-pumping excitement, high fives and dinners where we had one too many Old Fashions. Those contrast with days I break down in my car, scream and give my Toyota steering wheel an undeserved beating, soon followed by an apology and a car wash once the emotions leveled out. But the one thing that I have never faced is regret for my career choice.

I decided to write this book to share my experiences and the lessons I wish others had shared with me when I entered the world of consulting. It can be a minefield, and it is not for everyone. For every two coworkers I've seen succeed, I've seen one fail. It's an industry that will eat you alive if you don't know what you are doing or have the right mentorship in place. Unfortunately, a lot of firms do not have the right mechanisms in place for folks new to consulting and that is the gap I am hoping to close as best as I can with this book. Many experienced consultants will disagree with what I have written here, which, of course, is fair. Your goal as a new consultant is to gather as much information as you possibly can and make what you feel is the right decision for *you. Lesson one: you need to be able to defend your decisions.*

CONSULTING - A PRIMER

What is Consulting?

Consulting is defined by Wikipedia is as follows:

"A consultant (from Latin: consultare "to deliberate") is a professional who provides expert advice in a particular area such as security (electronic or physical), management, education, accountancy, law, human resources, marketing (and public relations), finance, engineering, science or any of many other specialized fields."

In this book, I define consulting as the Jack of All Trades, Master of Some. As a consultant, you might be contracted to fill a role an organization is unable to hire; you might be asked to be a subject matter expert to help solve a tricky problem. Consultants usually come at a premium based on experience, level and role and thus come with premium expectations as well. When things are right, a consultant is equipped with the right base knowledge, skill and tools to help clients solve their problems. The number one job of the consultant is to ask the right questions, find the right people to ask and create solutions to problems. No matter what anyone told you growing up, there are such things as stupid questions. Someone paying you over one hundred and fifty dollars an hour does not want to explain the basics of accounting to you. Consulting is either being the expert in the room or the person that is asking the right questions so that they may soon be the expert in the room. Being the latter—in the position of not knowing the details of something new—is nothing to fear. It is a common situation you find yourself in as a consultant. A good consultant will be able to learn and adapt quickly, earning themselves the title of the Jack of All Trades.

Why People Hire Consultants. The Math.

Consultants can usually run a rate of anywhere in the range of one hundred to two hundred dollars an hour. Some larger firms in the "Big Four" can charge up to six hundred dollars an hour for senior resources. Multiply that by the average of forty hours a week and fifty or so weeks a year, and it is easy to see how that adds up to more than you will see in your paycheck. Sorry to break it to you. What a consultant bills is never what they pocket in salary for reasons we will soon discuss.

When I first started consulting and reviewing my own billable rate, I could not even process how and why companies would pay that kind of money for someone like me. For that kind of money, companies could pay the salary of three or four versions of myself for the same period. It just did not add up.

There are a few major reasons most companies will hire consultants instead of hiring their own employees:

1. The work is project-based

The first major reason it makes sense for a company to hire a consultant is that the needed work must be completed in finite time with limited scope. Although the cost of the project can be high, a client will save thousands of dollars by not having to hire long-term, full-time resources. They can pay highly skilled, subject matter experts to come in and knock out the job. After completion, they can send the consultants on their way and transitioning the ongoing support to existing employees as a portion of their day job. The initial cost of the project is considered an investment with a long-term payback.

2. The work is temporary

Similar to project-style work, sometimes a company is simply short staffed. Maybe it is the year-end, maybe Mary is on maternity leave, and maybe they just need an extra hand hitting a deadline. In these cases, this work is usually called "Staff Aug," short for Staff Augmentation. Staff augmentation is where the current staff is supplemented by consultants for a limited time. The cost in this scenario is temporary because the role is temporary.

3. Consultants don't get benefits

The cost of a company's full-time employee exceeds his or her salary. Companies pay for the employee's desk, computer, parking pass, coffee, perks and—most importantly, the second most expensive item next to salary—benefits. With most reputable companies now offering retirement matches and health care benefits, the usual cost of an employee is over 20% beyond that person's salary. This is where the cost of hiring a consultant can begin to make a lot more sense.

4. The work is hard

Many times, a company will bring in a consultant because they just cannot do the work themselves. The work may be too complicated, or the organization may not have enough time or resources to complete the work on time or at all. Finding an expert to assist in complicated tasks is usually very hard to find and even more expensive to hire for the long-term. This is where specialty firms and their resources can flourish. Deep expertise in a business domain, an industry, or a technology drives most of the work for consulting firms.

5. The work is mandatory

Mandatory or regulatory work is where Big Four firms make much of their money. Audit season, Tax season, Merger and Acquisition reviews can be the reason you see an empty conference room get invaded by forty new folks dressed in the basic business casual starter kit and travel laptop. It is not rare to see these consultants working 80 hours a week, ordering take-out, hunching over documents and filling out spreadsheets. This type of work is necessary either by law/regulations or is required because of due diligence work. This is frequently where consultants get started.

How Consulting Works

For most of this book, I speak from the perspective of working for a consulting firm, not a staffing agency. A consulting firm usually hires, trains and invests in employees like any other company, while staffing agencies gear towards independent contractors and temporary staffing. A lot of valuable lessons in this book will also apply to the independent consultant. My experiences have not taken me down the solo consultant path, I wanted to avoid unfair assumptions.

A firm will hire you at a salary based on your skills, education and experience. The compensation structure is like any other job. You get paid every two weeks, with taxes and fees taken out of your paycheck and, if you are lucky, you make a bonus from time to time. This is the cost the firm incurs to hire an employee and is lovingly referred to as "employee burden" in company metrics.

The firm will staff its consultants on a client project. This is where the consultants get assigned to one of the many projects they have been contracted to deliver. As a member of this project team, the firm is "billing you out" at a certain rate per hour. This dollar amount, which varies based on the role, is collected at some cadence, usually monthly, when the firm invoices the client for the time and expenses billed in that timeframe.

All that cash collected in billing goes directly to the firm. It is this income that drives salary and bonuses, benefits, and perk as well as investment into employees and overall growth.

The Plumber and the Leaky Pipe

There is a classic story that really hits home the point of why consultants are necessary and why they can charge the rates they do.

There once was a man with a leaky pipe in his home. He attempted to repair the leak but could not figure out the solution, so he looked up a list of plumbers. He called the cheapest one first. The first plumber came by and after an hour of trying to solve the issue and failing, he charged the man fifty dollars for this time, apologized and left. The second cheapest plumber was then called. He also spent an hour looking for a resolution to solve the issue to no avail. He charged the man seventy-five dollars for this time, apologized and left. Frustrated, the man called the highest reviewed plumber over to his house. The new plumber showed up and listened to the man describe the issue. He then pulled out a wrench, opened a cabinet and tightened one bolt all within five minutes. The leak immediately stopped.

The plumber then turned to the man as said, "That will be two hundred and fifty dollars".

The man was appalled. "All you did was tighten one bolt? How can you charge that much?".

To which the plumber replied, "Because I knew exactly which bolt to tighten".

Key Metrics

Margin and Margin Percentage

The term "margin" is a key benchmark of a project's financial success. To put it simply, margin is the amount of profit earned on a project. To get to this number, you simply sum the revenue and subtract the cost. Margin's close friend "margin percentage" is simply margin divided by revenue. Margin percentage can be calculated at the individual consultant level, dividing the total revenue the consultant will generate and by total cost to keep that staff member employed (salary plus burden). This core calculation can be rolled up to projects, practices and the entire organization, and is a key metric related to a consulting firm's success.

Utilization

Utilization is frequently your key individual metric. The younger you are in your career, the higher likelihood this is the sole metric driving your performance reviews.

Utilization is the rate at which you were—you guessed it—utilized on a billable project. This metric is simple: it is the number of hours you billed divided by the number of hours you could have billed (usually 40). Some companies remove PTO (Paid Time Off) from the denominator as that will not count against you in the calculation. Either way works, as long as the company is consistent about it. Most firms target 75-95% of utilization, especially for their younger resources.

It is possible to go over a 100% utilization for weeks leading up to deadlines, but do not focus on exceeding 100% every week of your life. I have learned that is unsustainable and not a fair ask from your employer. If you are trying to make a name for yourself early on in your career, you will need to mix some of these long weeks in, but if your firm expects this of you consistently, they do not respect your personal and emotional wellbeing. You should probably prepare yourself for a more balanced position once you have the experience.

The combination of getting great margin and high utilization for younger resources is the key to why someone right out of school or early in their career is a great candidate for consulting firms. It's no secret that the salary of this type of person is going to be significantly less than someone with ten or more years' experience, which consequently means the core cost of that resource is also significantly lower. If this resource is billed out at the same utilization rate and similar billable rate as a highly experienced counterpart, their margin will be significantly higher. In short, the lowered salaried resource will generate more cash for the firm. Firms can offset this by charging a higher rate for managers, senior managers and above, but the margin increase by the higher rate tends to not offset rising salaries. To let you in on a little secret, firms are often looking for folks that are good learners to be jack-of-all-trades style employees at the entry-level. This allows them to capitalize on the high margins they produce.

Meeting Cost Calculator

As a consultant, be prepared to sit through a lot of meetings. You may even have meetings about meetings. A lot of time and money can be burned by sitting in these meetings and it will benefit you to keep tabs on how much a single meeting cost. Simply multiply the hourly rate of each resource by the attendees in the meeting. It is typical to have a one-hour meeting cost the client two thousand dollars. Knowing the cost will make you think twice about inviting too many attendees, meeting too frequently and letting topics meander.

Project Overrun

Project overrun is the cost incurred by the project running over time or budget. In fixed-bid projects or those where the client is unhappy, projects may require remediation (fancy term for "free work"), and may affect the profitability of your firm to eat up the cost of the overrun amount.

Fixed Bid Projects vs. Time and Material

Projects billed by the hour for the work performed are called "Time and Material" projects. This style of billing structure is where the cost of the work provided represents hours worked multiplied by the rate per hour of each resource. For example, if a consultant's rate is $100 per hour and they work 160 hours in a given month, they will bill the client $16,000. This is the most common method of project revenue as it allows an accurate representation of cost at a lower risk. Companies that usually hire consultants have some form of a project budget that cannot be exceeded without being seen as a failure. This dollar amount usually relates to the "return on investment" ("ROI") of the work, so it is in the firm's best interest to be honest and precise about initial estimates when scoping out the work. It also dissuades frivolous and inefficient billing.

Fixed bid projects represent a set cost project. This style of billing structure provides the client with a higher level of security against costs overrun. The contract usually includes specific deliverables for a set cost. From the consulting firm's perspective, it is in their best interest to staff this type of project to where the margin is similar to a time and materials project. If the project runs longer or burns at a higher rate, the margin decreases. If project finishes up sooner or requires fewer resource then the margin ends up being higher.

Independent vs. Firms

If you are an independent consultant, you are your own boss, working for yourself and keeping what you earn. Sounds great, right? It can be, but it comes with more risk. You will have to find your own work, pay your own benefits and pay self-employment tax. You are on the hook for your laptop, software, transportation, etc. (though you *do get to deduct them from your taxes).*

When you work for a firm, you are an employee of a larger machine. You are responsible for your day job and your daily tasks. The firm will pay your base salary and bonus, provide health care and benefits as well as provide you with the tools and training you need to perform. Firms have sales and support teams, HR, accounting and other necessary operational teams handling the "day to day" while you focus on your project work. They will bill you out at higher rates than you will find as an independent consultant, but most of those rates are kept by the firm to assist in paying your salary as well as operations costs required to run and grow a firm.

Compensation, Benefits and Pay Growth Expectations

The details of this section will vary wildly based on region, time, economy, firm size, role and a million other factors, but I wanted to create some high-level buckets you can plan around. Most of these are opinions from the perspective of working in North America, but the processes and structures will exist in most countries in similar capacities.

When it comes to compensation prior to even the interview process, remember to always do your research online to get a more accurate picture of what other consultants in similar roles are reporting. There are many websites that share salary ranges, reviews and possible interview questions which can be very valuable when looking for a new job. If you are entering consulting and are completely new to the field, with little to no experience, you are probably applying for the role of core entry-level consultant. Compensation can usually range anywhere around fifty to sixty thousand dollars a year right out of university. If you are lucky and the market is hot, you may be able to score a signing bonus as well that could potentially range from two to ten thousand dollars. Just remember, a signing bonus is considered income and will be taxable at the end of the year. Remember this before you blow more than 75% of your bonus on celebrating your new job.

The standard insurance benefits for a consulting role will include health care, dental care, vision, short-term disability and long-term disability. All the costs associated with insurance are rarely covered solely by your employer, but rather the cost is split between you and your employer where they pay the larger percentage and your cost portion will be deducted out of the bi-weekly paycheck. For benefits, you will be required to select the type of plan(s) when you are hired. After this, you will only be able to make changes during the insurance company's enrolment periods that usually occurs once a year for a few weeks, so choose wisely. Contact your HR or reach out to your provider to get all the information you require to ensure you get the right plans that fit you and your health needs.

On your first day, you will also be required to fill out a W-4 which can look complicated and overwhelming. The W-4 is a form that allows your payroll team to know how much money to withhold from your paycheck to cover year-end taxes owed. You will be asked to check off your allowances. The more you select, the less money will be withheld from your paycheck. However, if you do not withhold enough throughout the year, you may be on the hook for paying a large amount come tax season. Consult with your HR representative if you have any questions. The default best practice is to plan to have enough withheld so you do not have more to pay at the end of the year, while not having too much withheld to where you could have had that cash on hand for expenses and investments.

As you gain more experience, your pay will grow as well. This will be highly dependent on your performance reviews, the firm's financial performance and your decision to switch jobs. You should shoot for an average of between 3-10% pay increases every year. It is very common to break six figures within five-eight years of consulting, but you may also need to change firms every few years to get a better opportunity to negotiate a higher salary if your compensation bumps stalls out. I know job hopping can be frowned upon, but there is a difference between being loyal to a firm that respects you and pays your worth vs. one you are loyal to and is stunting your financial and personal growth.

Company Sizes

The Big Firm

You will occasionally hear the term "the big 5", which is a leftover term from the earlier days. Today, there are many players in the large consulting space. These firms span the globe with offices in most major cities and employ hundreds of thousands of folks. These companies recruit heavily out of college and you can probably find one of their recruitment booths at a school's career fair if you attend any major university.

Companies like these can be good choices for first-time consultants, as their onboarding and ramp up is geared toward low experienced hires. At a larger firm, you join the workforce alongside a series of your peers of a similar age, experience and mindset which can be a nice support structure as you learn the ropes. It is a good way to get a reputable name on your resume and is a great launching point for the rest of your career. This does not mean all hires come in through the college recruiting pipeline. Experienced hires are made at all levels of the organization to fill gaps or facilitate growth.

However, going to work at a big firm does come at a cost. Many big firms have the reputation of working their new hires long and hard hours. As an entry-level consultant, you are a high margin resource after all! If you are staffed, you are easily paying back the investment the firm has placed in you by helping to generate a significant revenue for the company. It is not unheard of to be working 50-70 hours a week at some of these firms. Many experienced employees will tell you that this is called "putting in your time". Be wary of being pushed too hard and too often and that you are not being taken advantage of or doing something you are uncomfortable with. If in doubt, reach out to your mentor or HR representative to discuss your concerns.

Large firms usually lead to and create an up or out culture. A healthy organization is shaped like a pyramid where the base is made up primarily of less experienced, cheaper and high margin resources, and as you go up through the organizational chart, the number of folk's decreases until you reach the C-level suite which is held by just a handful of employees. This is by design as it lines up with how to create the most effective and profitable type of company as higher experienced resources also cost more money to employ.

So, what does this mean for you? Are you on the chopping block every passing year? The answer for the most part is no. Natural attrition due to better pay, better roles and a thousand other reasons lead to most of the younger hires leaving the company for greener pastures. This is expected, so never feel bad about leaving if you have gotten your experience under your belt and have found a better opportunity. For the other half, many people enjoy working at these firms, the security they provide alignment to their personal career aspirations. For these folks, hitting your KPIs and making sure you network with your managers allows you to move higher in the organization towards that C-level suite. If you are good at what you do, you will usually see paths open up for you every two to three review cycles.

The Small Firm
Small firms are also known as the boutique firm. There are hundreds of thousands of these small businesses which range from two employees to about a hundred. Working for

the smaller firm has many pros and cons. Let's investigate some of the benefits first.

If you wish to work somewhere where your visibility and exposure to the client and your peers is high, then the small firm is the place to be. Everything you do will be seen by someone and it is a lot harder to hide behind your peers. Hopefully, this does not seem like a deterrent. This is actually a great place to be seen and recognized for your accomplishments much sooner as compared to a larger firm. Due to the size and volatility of the type of projects a small firm will be contracted to deliver, you will be required to learn and utilize a huge array of skills over a short period of time. Being early on in your career, this allows you to get first-hand experiences on a wide range of different projects and processes, letting you hone in on what you would really like to do going forward and naturally figure out your strengths and weaknesses.

The downside to working at the small firm all correlate to the positives we just mentioned. Since there is nowhere to hide, you are expected to perform at a higher level and learn a lot faster with less coaching and usually less training. Due to this, many people agree that working at a small firm can be significantly more stressful. These companies also come with a higher rate of employment risk. When large projects come to a close and cash flow dries up, there is not as much cushion to cover a bench. The smaller firm also may not have a dedicated sales team. As part of a small company, you may need to play the role of the sales person which means your core responsibilities could change day to day and that can be pretty scary.

In the end, the best type of company for you is the one that will align more with your personality and work style. If you like structure, well-planned direction and more security in your work, then bigger is better. If you like faster pace, more rounded experience and the ability to have more control of your career, then small is a better fit. If you're not sure and fall somewhere in between, then do not worry, there are plenty of middle-sized firms that have traits of both big and small and can vary depending on the style of the leadership and firms management.

Getting Hired

Getting hired at a consulting firm should not seem so scary. These firms want someone like you as much as you want to work for them. It makes financial sense to have a larger base of young, sharp employees that can make a killing on margin. Not a lot of experience is necessary or even expected. A lot of HR bragging stories you will hear revolve around "they picked these kids right out of school and they turned out to be rock stars". This also does not mean you can walk into a firm and expect them to be begging to hire you. You will need to prove you are a good fit, can pick things up really quickly, are ready to do the hard work and have the drive of wanting to succeed.

My First Consultant Job and Project

I ended up doing better on my second job interview then I did on my first. My honest and default answer to the ever-dreaded question "do you have experience in X" became "No, I do not but that is something I wish to learn". It was generic enough but it was true. Being 22, and not really having any hands-on experience, this was the only honest answer I could give. A small part of me felt ashamed and undeserving of the role but, little did I know, the HR recruiter on the other side was looking for just that answer. He saw my resume, he knew what I had done in the past yet he still called me. He was looking for someone that was relatively new. Based on the education, degree and other passions I had crammed into my one-pager, he saw someone he could hire fairly cheap; and believe me, he went for the lowball based on what I learned afterwards. All he needed to know was if I was capable of learning quickly, speaking confidently in front of a client and the willingness to put in time and effort to learn some new stuff. I was. I got my first job offer as a consultant joining a 6-person firm at the time that was mainly rooted in the pharmaceutical world. My first project landed me at a cosmetic company in Dallas and had me helping with a large system upgrade. My role was to help write hundreds of test scripts to ensure the newly designed system was working as expected. Embarrassingly enough, I wore oversized business casual clothes and spent the first 6 months of my career in a manufacturing plant storage room that had been converted into our consulting pit. It was scary, difficult and really, really cold all the time but it was where I started to learn the valuable lessons I hope to share in this book. Working at a cosmetic firm also led to many of my friends asking me if I sold make-up and which eyeliner I preferred.

Resumes

Getting your resume clean and prepared is going to be the first step to getting hired on as a consultant. Colleges usually offer resume writing help for current students, but if this is not an option for you, there are plenty of templates you can find online. The usual advice you will hear for resumes is to keep it to one page, but I have rarely seen a one-pager in a long time. There is no issue in having a resume that is two to three pages long if the experience you are listing is relevant. My personal one is pushing four pages and that is with a lot of less important roles trimmed off.

On the header, you will want to have all your basic information: Name, address and email. Please be sure to create a professional email if you do not have one. John.Smith@mail.com will read a lot better than dragonlord@mail.com.

In the summary section, the key bullets you will want to hit very quickly are your years of experience for anything valuable that will set you apart. Anything else in the summary section that contains phrases like "hard working, attention to detail, etc." are often ignored or skimmed over as everyone uses them. Just avoid spelling errors and keep it brief.

In the next section, list out only your post high school education. No need to list your elementary school or high school. If your GPA was reputable (above 3.0), be sure to mention that next to your degree. Once you cross about 5 years' experience, the education section can be bumped to the back of the resume.

The following section is the most important. Experience is where most recruiters and interviewers jump right into. Be sure to list these in chronological order, starting with the most recent going backwards. You are applying to a detail and task-oriented position when looking at consulting roles, so be sure to format your resume to fit such a mold where possible. Even if you have only worked in retail, there are key ways to highlight your task-based skills:

Retail Store (2012-2014)

- Responsible for daily inventory count and reconciliation
- Responsible for weekly scheduling
- Assisted with new hire training and mentoring

Let's take a quick look at what messaging this conveys to a potential recruiter. The first thing the recruiter will notice is that you spent two years at the role. This shows you are willing to put in the time and stay committed to your job. No one likes a job hopper. Second, a lot of projects are detail-oriented and based on numbers, tallies and totals. Being able to demonstrate you have experience in seeing and adhering to a process is a big plus. The next bullet point focuses on creating structure and organization. This has tangents to many things you will be doing as an entry-level consultant. The last point demonstrates that you are a team player, and you show the willingness to invest in other employees and the company as a whole. It also shows that you have people skills and communication skills.

In any final section of your resume, choose between special projects you may have accomplished in school, certifications or both. Outside of these primary categories, the rest is a careful balance between valuable information and fluff. Remember that you are selling yourself to a complete stranger through writing. Use these basic tips and show it to as many friends and professionals in your network for proofreading prior to sending out.

The Case Study Interview
The case study job interview is where the applicant is given a scenario or situation and asked to present a solution by detailing all the steps and processes the applicant would need to put into place. The scenarios are usually a business case but sometimes are off the wall questions that involve filling empty rooms with quarters or determining the best way to move a rock up a hill with only a few tools. In the case interview, more than just the creativity of the final solution, the interviewer is looking to evaluate your thought process, your problem-solving skills under pressure and your ability to logically formulate a solution and present your findings.

The Wrong Answer Case Study

As I was interviewing at large consulting firms, I entered a case study interview feeling confident having just nailed the one on one portion. Three current employees sat down directly in front of me, forming a panel. It was clear they were younger than I was and had been drinking the company Kool-Aid. They wore matching company embroidered polos and haircuts to match. They went on to inform me what a privilege it was for me to even be in the same room as them and how I would be lucky to work there if I made it through their case study. After presenting a scenario centered around airport security lines and tasked with detailing a new process to increase the efficiency of the lines, they comforted me by informing me there were no wrong answers to the problem and they just wanted to hear my thought process and problem-solving skills. After thirty minutes of being left alone and creating what I thought was a pretty solid plan on the white board, they reentered the room and I presented my solution which could have 'no wrong answer'. They immediately told me my answer was incorrect and proceeded to show me their "correct" solution. I realized then that some case study interviews are unwinnable. They are based on a subjectivity and bias of the interviewer. It turns out I was "not a good fit" for the company a few days later but I had already come to that conclusion myself after exiting the case study interview.

CONSULTING 101

Optics

Being a consultant is not just about the work you do. How you are perceived is a big part of your job. This is where consulting differs from just having an industry job. Consultants will need to work hard to be perceived as a hard-working expert. Once you finally achieve that goal, the project will end and you will roll off on to another project where the process will begin again.

Coming in early or leaving late is usually a good way to be seen as a hard-working individual but it is also a good way to burn yourself out. Try to pick one or the other if you can, and either be the guy that stays late or the guy that is always the first in the office. Earlier in my career, it was always easier to stay late and be the night owl. As I got older, it fit my schedule better to be one of the first ones into the office. If I had to pick between the two, coming in earlier seems to be the better option when it comes to what looks better to a client. It also allows for plenty of time to relax and decompress in the evening before the next day begins.

Try to do a frequent health check on the image you are putting forward, whether it be your attire, your work ethic or how much time you spend chatting with others in the break room. The perception that client has of you will be a major factor in your ongoing work.

Attire

Attire is a pretty complicated topic, and by no means am I a fashion expert. Fashion trends tend to change year to year, so what may be in style at the time of writing this book, may make me seem like the uncool dad by the time you are reading this. Instead, I wanted to talk about some of the unchanging rules of dressing for your consulting job. The ultimate rule is to always dress better than your client. That does not mean for you to wear a full suit if their general attire is very casual as you don't want to create a large disparity, but it is recommended you stick to the basics of business casual. Always remember you are supposed to be the expert in the room and your personal image is a part of that. A big part of your professional image is rooted in the fact that you are always selling. You are selling the firm, your work and yourself, so how you present yourself directly influences your goals.

Coming out of college, it can be very difficult to know what is acceptable and, more importantly, what is affordable. Dressing well can get very pricey but there are ways to save a few bucks and look good. Look online and check blogs for what is considered business casual and business formal. The basics of what classifies have not changed drastically over the years. What has changed are colors, fit and cut. Once you have an idea of what looks you are shooting for, go to your local mall and try to figure out what fits well and what you are comfortable with. Once you have a good baseline of the look you are going for and your basic size, you should be able to start building your wardrobe. Designer labels are nice but they are not necessarily a good choice if you are on a budget. How clothes fit and look are usually more important than the brand. You should be able to shop online or at department stores to always look for sales on work clothes. You can always mix and match tops, bottom and shoes to create new outfit combinations out of a fewer number of items. If your personality is loud, don't be scared to express some of that as long as you stay within the bounds of business casual. If you wish to stick to the dark greys, blues and black for the first few months or years to blend in until you're comfortable, there is nothing wrong with that either. Keep an eye out for veteran peers to get a good pulse on what goes and what does not.

As a basic rule of thumb, tattoos and piercings should be covered up or removed. Although some of these are permanent decisions and expressions that are a part of you, it is easier to keep them covered as the attention should focus on the skills you were hired to share and not on your body art.

What Does My Client Do?
The very first thing you must learn before you set foot through a client's front door is the basic understanding of what they do, their goals and how they generate revenue. Initial insight can be found on the company's website under their mission statement or the "about us" section. Dig through their entire public facing website to get a good idea of what image they are promoting to their customers. Even

though this image may not match what you see when you hit the ground, it will give you a good idea of what they originally wanted to be or what they plan to grow into. Most companies fall into some basic industry like pharmaceuticals, banking, telecom, etc., so it is wise to read through the basic Wikipedia articles on how those industries came about, how they currently exist and how they generate their revenue and growth. Your client may be more of a niche player in a larger industry, but knowing the bigger picture is always a good start. From the high-level, dig into the specific goals and revenue models of the respective client. Most of your valuable discoveries will come once you are onsite but this should give you a good head start and allow you to speak with more credibility early on. The last item you will want to research is the exact group you will be working with and the basics of their day job. Will you be working with accounting? Read a basics of accounting book. Are you going to be helping review data for a private equity firm? Pick up some books on how PE Firms operate and invest. If you get stuck finding information or want to know more, reach out to your manager or mentor and see if they can guide you to some resources at your firm.

Questions and How to Ask Them

A consultant's job is to create answers and asking a good question is the number one tool you have in your consultant's tool belt to get those answers. As you try to figure out the hidden problems and the clever solutions, you will be interviewing your clients in what are called requirement gathering meetings. Below are some high-level guidelines you can follow to be sure you're getting the most out of your client requirement sessions:

1) Bring something to write with. This is imperative. A notebook, a laptop or a tablet are acceptable and put your college training to good use and take notes while listening to a flowing conversation. Information will come at you fast, so be prepared.
2) Start by first asking what core problem they are trying to solve. If you already know what the answer is, restate your assumptions and ask the group to validate. Starting with questions to why you are there and lining up high-level expectations is a good place to start.
3) Ask questions that will give you a good general understanding of the client's role, their responsibilities and how they intersect with the goals previously discussed.
4) It is ok to ask the client to repeat something that was missed or was unclear. You will not catch or comprehend everything the first time it is spoken.
5) Keep digging to get the answers you are looking for. Remember, clients are usually explaining something they do day in and day out and will either gloss over valuable details or assume that are familiar with. Follow-up questions should explore deeper into topics and be targeted to getting to the core answers you need.

6) Do not ask the same question for multiple days or meetings to the same person. It is completely fair to ask for further clarification on a previous topic if you are stuck, but if you have just forgotten, then you need to be taking better notes the first time around. This can ruin your credibility as a good listener and attention to detail. Asking the same question to another client team member is fair game, however, as the misalignment in the answers may represent the misalignment in the business you are attempting to discover.
7) It is always helpful to repeat back what you heard and ask if your understanding of something is accurate. You may misinterpret a response and catching it early on is always best.
8) Unfortunately, there are such things as dumb questions. As previously mentioned, the more research you can do prior to landing on site, the better shape you will be in. It will be expected of you to have some core level of skill, expertise and competency, so be sure to do your homework.

I can Teach it to You, but I cannot Understand it for You

One of the biggest frustrations you will have as a consultant will be in trying to explain a concept or an idea to another and them not being able to grasp it. You may even be reminded of the quote, "if you cannot teach it, you probably do not understand it well enough", but that quote does not always hold true. Some of us are not good teachers or explainers by nature, which is why we never choose teaching as a career. There are some basic skills you can brush up on to assist with the art of teaching:

1) Always start at the beginning of the subject and define what it is. Even if the audience is familiar with the topic, setting a baseline of basic understanding is a good idea. Remember to be respectful and do not be condescending as there are many things in life you do not know and will need to be taught.
2) Give examples and use the white board to illustrate when you can. A lot of people are natural visual learners. Helping draw out examples and concepts will help with comprehension and will facilitate the listeners to ask counter questions that will aid them in connecting the dots.
3) Switch gears if you get stuck. There is nothing more frustrating than not understanding something and having the teacher just repeat the same thing over and over, hoping it just clicks. Sometimes a fresh approach or analogy will help do the trick.
4) Assist with analogies outside of the subject area. Bringing in outside references that the listener may be familiar with could help. They do not even need to be directly related to the topic. If you can explain half the idea using a baseball comparison and the second half using football rules, combining the two into some new magical sport, there is nothing wrong with that as long as you can pull the tangent

back to the original topic and assist with comprehension.

Quick Wins and How to Say No

In client services, the ability to go above and beyond is not just necessary, it is a must. Just floating by and doing the bare minimum may be enough to successfully complete the items listed in the statement of work, but your ultimate goal should always be on winning the next set of follow-up work. One of the best ways to do this is by delivering slightly more than what your client originally signed up for. Growing existing clients rather than finding new ones is the easiest way to win work for your firm and it is the job of the team on the ground to ensure that happens.

As requirements evolve and the project ebbs and flows, you will have the opportunity to take on new additional items that may either be an extension of the existing scope or tangential. Tasks that can be done in a relatively short period of time and not impact or impede the overall project plan are called quick wins.

The ability to spot a good quick win vs. what would not be worth the effort is where the ability to say no to a client intersects. Clients can and will ask you to take on additional work all the time and it will be up to you and your project manager to decide whether the extra effort will be worth it in the long run. Usually, if the item is low effort and high reward, it is a safe bet to take on the extra item. It will be perceived well by the client and not add too much risk to your existing project. As the work increases in complexity and lowers in terms of the reward it carries for the client, this is where it is wise to begin pushing back on the client. Maybe you could push the work to another future phase, or carefully explain the work vs. the impact. You will need to learn to say no to a client from time to time. Whether the client is innocent in asking for additional items or they are purposely pushing the team to get more bang for their buck, this is where scope creep can begin to put your project at risk. It will be down to you and your project manager to manage expectations.

Saying No and Finding a Compromise

A client once approached my desk, rolled up a chair and sat down next to me. As I removed my headphones and turned from the task I was currently working on, he started to engage in some quick small talk. As I listened to a story about his dog, I knew he was on track to pivot to a requirement change. Clients that need a quick change usually avoid project management and go directly to the developer in hopes of getting what they want. "Oh, I believe it's simple, but I would be grateful if we could also have the tool to do so and so..."

I let him know his request was fair and I would look into feasibility while knowing that the change being requested would add a lot of work to my plate as well as derail the task I was currently working on. Once he left, I reported the task back to my project manager who recorded the item to the backlog. At the next status meeting, we brought up the new item with all parties being present and quickly decided that the new item was worth the effort and the current task I was working on could be bumped to a later phase. In this scenario, the client gave up a bit but also got something he wanted, and I did not have to double time it to produce more work. Win-Win.

Scope Creep

"Can you please add a new order management screen for international orders...?" or "Can you please write up the quarterly close process since you are already doing the monthly process?" There are a million ways a client will ask you to do a bit more than what you signed up for. Sometimes these are just different interpretations of the original requirement and sometimes they are completely new requests. One way or another, they grow your scope and they will impact your timelines. It can be very hard to catch this early on, especially in the early phases with new clients. Scope creep is one of the major reasons a project will go over time and over budget. Catching scope creep is an easier task when major items are being added or changed in flight, but it is the small ones that sneak under the radar that you need to watch out for. Doing small changes every now and then can add up to a lot of extra time and effort spent in the long run.

Scoping the Work Correctly
Nine women cannot make a baby in one month. When staffing projects and analyzing the work that needs to be completed there is a common fallacy that if you throw more bodies at the work, it will get completed faster. You will find this does not always hold true. Although there are some situations where the work load can be split up and delegated to multiple resources to complete sooner, there are many situations where due to dependencies or the natural rate or flow of a project, adding more resources will not accelerate the work. In fact, this will only increase your burn down initially leaving less time and budget down the road. It is best to evaluate how long each work item will take and what the core requirements are. Sometimes it is better to go slower at a comfortable pace rather than try to dash at the beginning. This can add risk for everyone as the project continues. In the book The *Mythical Man Month*, author Frederick Brooks cements the point that "adding manpower to a late software project makes it later". Scoping work accurately is an art and will take some time to learn. Use more senior resources for guidance and feedback when available.

Under Promise, Over Deliver
You will hear this phrase numerous times on many different clients and it is a part of every consultant's motto. There is nothing wrong or unethical about committing to work you know will be feasible to accomplish in the given time and will not require additional stress and extra hours. This is

where the difference lays between under promising and sandbagging, the latter is frowned upon and considered an unethical practice as you would be working at a slower pace to drag out work and billable hours. Under promising allows you to set commitments with the client that you are confident are winnable in your favor, similar to playing a game where you set the odds in your favor.

Overpromising creates unnecessary risk and additional work, thus creating scope creep. It can put you and your firm's reputation on the line by setting the client's expectation to tasks that you may not be able to complete on time or at all. It is always best to avoid overpromising work by analyzing the work against the quick win criteria.

If you can over deliver in the same time-frame of the existing project plan, without burning too much extra time or burning yourself out, then giving the client a bit more than they originally expected is always a welcome surprise. Going above and beyond for a client will always be appreciated and will help put you on the path for selling future work and additional phases of projects.

Land and Expand

A common sales tactic used by consulting firms is where the project team or the group continues to drive new work and opportunity. This is called land and expand. This method of growth is the lifeblood of all successful firms as it costs more and takes far longer to get a new client through the door than it does to continue work or expand work for an existing client. As you work, be sure to keep an eye and ear out for new needs. The ability to identify new opportunities is usually not very difficult. Most of it will organically fall on your lap as the client requests new items to add to existing requirements or as unknown tasks are discovered once the work begins. Be sure to work with your project manager to track and catalog these items as they come up. The client may try to force your hand into knocking some of these out in your current scope of work, but be sure to properly weigh the benefits of these and see if any fall into the category of quick wins, as previously mentioned, or if they can be positioned as future work.

Usually, your project work with one business unit will begin to open up connections and needs in other parts of the business. Projects in accounting may begin to intersect with operations. Operations may uncover gaps in the technical systems. Growing projects horizontally across the organization will allow you to grow a stronger foothold at the client. Different business units will often carry their own budgets which means there is more money on the table for your firm to win. Winning revenue for your firm is one of the best ways to get noticed and promoted!

Ethics and Lying

When you play the role of the consultant, you are usually expected to be the expert in everything. In reality, you will be placed in situations where things are very new to you. This is where the fine line between being a professional and outright lying can be difficult to navigate. Many times, your sales team will sell you and your role to a client without any outside input and you will be the one left on the hook to deliver the expectations they set. It would be easy to just tell everyone a few white lies to cover for yourself until you can sort things out, but that can and will land you in hot water pretty quickly. Remember, you are usually with the client who probably has some fundamental knowledge of his or her own day job and will be quickly able to figure out if you are making statements that you won't be able to back up.

Since the situation of not always being the expert you were sold as is usually unavoidable from time to time, it is best to talk about what to do in this situation rather than really spend a lot of time talking about how to avoid it. In these situations, it is a good strategy to hide behind a wall of questions rather than a wall of lies. Asking the right questions is rarely seen as a lack of understanding and, in fact, can show your ability to connect dots, build rapport and give you the opportunity to get your footing and become the expert you are expected to be. Prior to walking into the client's home turf, remember to do as much research as you can. Between searching the internet, the sales teams' notes and your firms' management, there is a wealth of information you should be able to gather. Research what the client does on their company website. Are you going to be working with their accounting department? The sales and marketing group? Read through some self-paced courses on the topic as there are plenty of free sources online. Ask your manager if there is any in-house training you could take prior to starting with the client. It is also vital for your manager to sit down with you before going onsite and discuss the details and responsibilities of the work that was signed off. If you are being sent to the wolves to fend for yourself with no support, it would be wise to raise that concern early as it is not a situation that will send you or your firm on a path to success.

Another big ethics violation you may encounter revolves around accurately recording and reporting hours worked. A great motto to live by is: "bill what you work". If your manager or director is trying to artificially inflate your billable hours, that will be an automatic red flag. This is a cash grab and any ethical-based firm will not allow this. This action is also a breach of contract and could land your firm in legal hot water. Some firms usually try to mask this by suggesting you actually work 45 to 50 hours a week. If there is work to be done and you are trying to stay ahead of schedule or build a name for yourself, it is usually ok. However, if you are finding yourself watching videos online or scrounging for ways to kill time without producing anything valuable, it would be wise to raise this concern as it counts as taking advantage of the client. In certain situations, you may see the opposite of hour inflation where you actually work a valid number of extra hours but your manager is not billing that time in an effort to keep the project under budget. This situation helps no one in the long run and you lose a lot of credit and merit for the difficult work you may be doing. In these situations, your manager should be allowing you to record the true hours you worked so that there is a digital record of the true hourly cost. The manager can then mark the hours worked as non-billable time to the client so there is no financial cost incurred. This would be at your leadership's discretion but allows you to be credited for the hours you put in while showing the client the actual work being done. This, in turn, keeps the billable run rate down if the work is not actually being billed.

Something Does Not Feel Right

In one of my earlier projects working for a smaller firm, I was sold to a client as someone more experienced than I really was at the time. That should have been my first warning sign, but not wanting to make a fuss and being young at the time, I went forward with the role. After a few weeks of staring at an empty screen and rereading the same documents to appear busy, I only billed the hours I was actually working. I was told after a few weeks by my employer that I should bill fifty hours no matter what. That was strike two. As the weeks went on, the project failed to deliver anything useful and my current manager was stalling on purpose. The client began to get angry and took their frustrations out on the consultants on the ground and threatened to take my employer to court for the fees they were charged and the lack of deliverables to show for it. I wish I could tell you how this story ends, but at this point, I knew something was not right and this was not how ethical firms would behave or ask their employees to behave, so I quit and moved on to a better opportunity at a firm I felt was led by better people.

The War Room/Consulting Pit

When working onsite, some clients will set you up with your own cubicle workspace, but when teams are bigger or space is more limited, you will probably end up in what is called the war room or the consulting pit. This space is usually an unused conference room or open area with a few large tables where you and your team will be set up. Do not be shocked to find internet wires running wild, connected to routers strewn across the floor. I've been in consulting pits that range from 3 people in an old storage room of a manufacturing plant to a conference room with twelve people sitting shoulder to shoulder. This space also lends itself to a lot of good collaboration and ease of asking your fellow coworkers questions and helping to provide answers. Be aware and respectful of others, however, as frequent interruptions and constant talking may be a bother to them. Be mindful of the volume from multiple loud conversations since the conversation could bleed out to the hallways where other employees may be sitting. If you do need to have broader conversations, see if an executive assistant can help you find an unused conference room for thirty minutes to an hour where you can speak more freely.

Try to keep this space organized and clean. Remember, you are using borrowed space and are expected to respect it as you would your own home and office. Do not leave trash sitting around and also be sure to remove or shred any sensitive client data. This room can get very frustrating and uncomfortable at times but a lot of the nostalgic moments of your career will come from the hours spent in these consulting pits.

Imposter Syndrome

As time passes and you get more experience under your belt, you will find yourself answering questions and leading meetings like you have been working in the client's industry for decades. At this point, as you self-reflect on the flight back home, you may get hit with a feeling of anxiety known as imposter syndrome. What makes you the expert? Are you really as knowledgeable as everyone thinks you are? Am I an imposter, a fraud, a con man? A Jack of No Trades, a Master of None...just faking it and fooling everyone at a billable rate I do not deserve. This feeling is common in many consultants due to the high velocity required to switch roles and learn new businesses, processes and technologies. It is completely normal to feel the self-doubt and the inability to appreciate your own skill and knowledge. In consulting, when you start a new project, you will have to dance the dance while you get comfortable and get your feet under you, but drawing the line of when you transition from not knowing to knowing can create a false insecurity from time to time. Remember to take a step back and give your skills of a smart, adaptive and creative consulting credit for being as good as they really are.

Dealing with the age gap
The earlier you are reading this in your career, the larger the age gap you may encounter between those that have hired you to consult them. This can create some awkward situations and conversations. There will be a difference in thought process and opinions just based on the generational differences alone. Always remember to be respectful and humble to the wisdom of others. Even though there might be situations where you may or do know best, understanding and appreciating others will only benefit you in the long run.

Many times, you will be implementing some form of new technology to help replace or assist older manual processes and tools. These newer technologies may be foreign to the people you are working with, in the same way learning their existing process is foreign to you. Remember to exercise patience when explaining and training and use some of the skills you learned on how to teach others effectively. A little empathy will go a long way. Many of these people have been doing the same task, the same way for many years and change will be scary to them.

There will be times that fighting for respect with an age gap difference is a losing battle. Having to take advice and orders from someone thirty years younger may be too much for someone's ego. In these scenarios, it is ok to let your manager know and work with your team to take a possible back seat on client facing scenarios and pick up the slack somewhere else. For example, you can be the one that takes notes at a meeting with the client and have another team member conduct the interview portion. Ideally, after some time, you will be able to forge a better relationship with your client once you have demonstrated your skills and value and be able to take more of a leading role on the client facing side.

New Kid on the Block

I was essentially younger then the pictures of Doug's grandchildren that sat on his desk. The piece of database code he was walking me through had been written before I had even entered high school. As Doug spoke, I felt pretty uncomfortable knowing I had been hired to replace items he had owned and worked on for nearly thirty years, but Doug was always kind and very happy to answer any question I had. As I reflected back, I was pretty grateful for having a subject matter expert who was eager and patient enough to explain something he had done a million times over and could do in his sleep. As the project ended and we completed a round of development that automated and replaced a lot of items that Doug normally did, something strange happened. He actually got busier. The items we had helped him with had freed up his time to do larger and more important things for the company he had helped build. Overall it was a very rewarding experience for me and it seemed it had been for him as well.

Water Cooler Talk

Not all your conversations are going to revolve around work and work-related items. Many times, as you relax and build personal relationships with your coworkers and clients, the topics will swing to non-work-related conversations. Connecting at a personal level is vital to your success in your career and is encouraged. There are a few important items to remember when this is occurring during work hours:

1) Don't go overboard on time. Remember you are billing by the hour. Try to keep these conversations quick and light and not drag out for more than 10 minutes. If you get caught with a long-winded talker, just politely check your watch and let them know you have an important item to get back to and will catch up with them after-hours.

2) There is no need to be an expert in everything. You may not be a big football fan or a fan of a particular TV show. There is no need to pretend just to fit in, this is not high school. If there is a conversation topic you are not familiar with, ask questions to get involved. Who knows, this may be the start of discovering something new to do in your spare time.

3) Avoid conversations about politics and religion. The workplace is not a safe place for these as many people can have very strong and opposing opinions that differ from yours and can make for uncomfortable situations. It is best to excuse yourself or remain silent if someone is trying to draw you into a conversation around these topics.
4) You will need to have a good level of self-awareness when discussing personal topics. Asking about someone's pregnancy or family, health is usually not a first day kind of conversation and takes time to build up a good personal relationship where this would be considered fair conversation. If you have to ask yourself, "I wonder if this would offend him/her," then it's best to play it safe and say nothing at all.

Cursing

Cursing has been shown in many studies to have all kinds of benefits. It relieves stress and can help numb pain when you're physically hurt. People that curse are often perceived as more honest, and it can help build comradery. However, it can also be perceived as crude, offensive, rude, brash and hurt people's feelings. If cursing is a part of your verbal repertoire, it is still good to keep the language professional and toned down when dealing with client and coworkers while the relationship is new. As relationships grow and become more comfortable, take your cues from others on what is acceptable or not. If your boss drops the occasional

F-bomb, it is probably ok to do the same as the situation allows. With clients, always try to show more restraints, but if your client is cursing like a sailor and even makes you blush from time to time, it is probably ok to engage.

Under no circumstances are slurs ever acceptable and it probably does not make you a great person if you really need to use such offensive language.

Discussing Race, Religion, Politics, Sexual Orientation
Don't. Just Don't.

Email Etiquette
Outside of direct conversation, your primary means of communication is going to be via digital email. When writing emails, be sure to be clear and concise.

1) Reread your email before sending it. Always check for spelling and grammatical errors.
2) If you are sending the email with an attachment, double check you actually attached the file. It's always slightly embarrassing to get a quick reply back asking if you forgot your attachments.
3) Always be polite and courteous in your greeting and send off. Your emails represent you and your image, so be sure to give them a professional look and feel.

4) If the email is going to be very long, there is a chance it will not get read all the way through or skimmed by the reader. Try to include a summary at the top or list out your major points in bullet points to get them across to the email skimmers.
5) If you are expecting a reply back or require action items, be sure to list them out and tie names and dates to them if needed.
6) If replying back to a single person, always double check you did not hit 'reply all'. If you need to send a sensitive personal message and do not want to risk everyone accidentally being sent the email, take a few extra seconds to create a brand-new email to avoid getting your wires crossed.
7) Be sensitive to other peoples' time. Email notifications can be a large distraction and getting a little chime on your screen every few minutes can really hinder someone else's productivity. Similar to walking over and tapping them on the shoulder, be cognizant of the distraction an email may cause and only send if really necessary or group a few together if they logically make sense too.

Emails can sometimes work against you and waste more time than they save. If a conversation goes on for more than three emails, ask yourself if it is better to just pick up the phone and have a conversation. Sometimes nothing beats a good person to person conversation.

The Internet is Forever

Somethings in life you don't get to take back. An inappropriate email sent companywide is one of those things. Onsite at a multinational oil and gas conglomerate, writing some code, I saw a ping from my email informing me that I had received an email to my client inbox folder. Usually, emails to this folder were companywide updates that did not really concern me, but seeing that the subject had a series of forwards and a reference to the sitting president at the time, I decided to open it. The body of the email read a crude joke that hit on race, politics, gender and religion. The ultimate superfecta of office no-nos. I guessed the sender had a friend named Albert or Allister, but she mistakenly sent the email to "All Employees". This email was soon followed by another message from compliance asking everyone to delete the email and apologizing for the content of the email. I can only imagine the embarrassment the sender felt and would be surprised if that was not her last day on the job.

Offshoring

Many firms use a practice called offshoring. Offshore resources on a project are team members who are located in a different country overseas or in a different continent. Offshoring is often used as a method to get work done for a client at a significantly lower cost. Usually, resources who work in another country outside North America have lower salary requirements due to the lower cost of living. Another big benefit of offshore resources is that it allows projects in North America to keep running after-hours since the team overseas is usually in a different time zone. Because of this, offshore resourcing works great in roles that require after-hours technical support, monitoring or development that does not require too much interaction with the core local team.

Dealing with offshore resources does come with its challenges, however. There are many cultural and language barriers that must be overcome when dealing with resources in another country. Most are often English speaking but did not learn English as a primary language. There are many things that can get lost in translation. Expectation for average daily work hours and general ethics vary from region to region. Some cultures proudly work for 12 hours a day while others have afternoon naps and many holidays and celebrations that need to be planned around.

When dealing with passing off requirements and direction to an offshore team, be sure to be clear and concise. Many development teams will follow your direction to a "T" and not make the same logical assumptions you would. Setting expectations early on both sides and having management oversee the work from onshore is critical to being able to use offshore successfully.

Onsite and Offsite Locations

An Onsite location represents the actual location of the client or one of their offices. Work that needs to be completed onsite will have you traveling to the client's onsite office where you will be set up with a desk or consulting pit to work from. Offsite locations represent any location where work can be completed away from a client's location. This can be your firm's office, your home or even a local coffee shop. Determining where you will work will usually be left to the client's preference as some feel more comfortable with boots on the ground onsite, where others are more flexible or do not have work space and prefer you to work from your own location.

Working Remote

If a project allows you to work remote, it means they do not mind where you conduct your work from. You can work from your local office or you can work from home. Anywhere that has a nice stable internet connection as well as a quiet place to take a phone call will suffice. Since actual client visibility is low when you are working remote, it is best to be extra diligent on sending status updates and keeping on top of your work items. Be extra communicative to help confirm the perception that you are working and completing your tasks. Since you will not be onsite to sell yourself as much, compensate by selling good work and clean communication to make up for it.

Never Burn a Bridge and saying Goodbye

Everyone you meet and work with is a possible future client, coworker or friend. Keep this in mind as you wrap up client engagements. Even if a project was rocky or had you working long hours, be sure to leave on a good note with a good impression. When work pops up later, you want to be on the short list of people they call. It's easy to give a bad client the bird as you walk out but that small moment of self-satisfaction is not worth the value of what may come later on. Your network is a spider's web of potential. You never know who may know who or who went to school with someone else's wife's best friend that can lead to a project, job or opportunity ten years down the line.

Consulting Key Phrases

50-Thousand-Foot View
The 50-thousand-foot view of an item or process is when you take a step back and only look at the high-level aspects of it. Many people will get lost in the minutia of an item or begin to jump down rabbit holes when trying to explain something, so it is good to bring the conversation back up to a higher level when that is all that is needed.

Low Hanging Fruit
Low hanging fruit describes tasks or project items that are very simple and quick to accomplish. These tasks can be started and completed from beginning to end. A good

consulting strategy will stack a series of low hanging fruit at the beginning of phases of work so that the client can see the immediate benefits of the work.

Let's Circle Back Around to That

This phrase will occur in two instances. The first is when the conversation has spiraled out of control or taken a tangent and what is being discussed is not immediately valuable to the original conversation. Noting down this tangent and coming back to it at a later time is sometimes the best course of action to ensure you don't go too far off track. The second scenario this will occur in is when the audience member is lost in the conversation or does not have an immediate answer. This is a good way to get a break in the conversation on a topic you may not be familiar with and give yourself some time to get familiar with the topic so you do not discredit yourself.

Boiling the Ocean

The metaphor of boiling the ocean represents trying to do too much at once. Taking on more than you can chew adds risk and creates a larger amount of work that may be too much to handle with results that take too long to surface.

Peeling the onion

Peeling the onion describes the process of breaking down a business process one layer at a time, starting from the top.

Sticker Shock

Sticker shock is when you present the client with the statement of work you have been working on for a few weeks and they freak out due to the high price tag. The client may not realize initially what average consulting rates are these days or being shocked by the amount of work or the duration of work. Before presenting a statement of work, it is best to review and discuss with your internal team. There may be room for negotiation if you are trying to get a foothold at the client for an eventual land and expand strategy.

SOW (Statement of Work)

The SOW is the detailed document that defines the project purpose, requirements, effort, hours and cost that the client would incur if the project is initiated. A signed SOW by both sides (the firm and the client) is when a project is considered "Inked" and official.

RFP (Request for proposal)

This is a document that requests agents and firms to submit their bid or statement of work for a set of initial requirements.

Non-Disclosure Agreement (NDA)
A non-disclosure agreement is a legal contract between at least two parties that list confidential material, knowledge, or information that the parties wish to share with one another for certain purposes, but wish to restrict access to or by third parties. An NDA is usually created and signed between the client and consulting organization early in the sales process so that both parties may discuss the problem area the client is having as well as the solutions the consulting firm can offer.

Master Services Agreement (MSA)
A Master Services Agreement is a contract reached between parties, in which the parties agree to most of the terms that will govern future transactions or future agreements.

Sensitive Data
You should always treat your client's data as sensitive even if no one explicitly mentions it. If you are working for a banking or government client, strict rules will probably be laid out for you once you join the team, but if no one mention's the level of security needed, it is always best to be responsible and respectful to the documents and data the client has shared with you. When you walk away from your computer, be sure to lock the screen and set a password to log back in. If you have physical documents you no longer need, find the nearest shredder to ensure the documents are disposed of correctly. When using physical

media to transfer files, install encryption software on your computer and make sure files are secure in case you lose your portable hard drive.

How to get Fired from a Project

Bob was a team member of mine who always needed to leave slightly early to pick up his kids and then would work the rest of the evening from his home office. One day when he was in the middle of a comparing data for a banking client, he decided to email the file to his personal email so he could download the file at home and continue his work. Little to his knowledge, the file contained social security numbers. Once the email was sent, network security was immediately notified, followed by the authorities. Bob was confronted by the client the very next morning and escorted out of the building. This policy breach was a non-negotiable offense and required immediate termination. It is probably safe to say that Bob will always thinks twice before emailing sensitive data to himself.

Office Space Etiquette

Your Desk

Whether you are granted your own workspace or you are set up in a consulting pit, how you maintain your designated space reflects on you and the image you are creating at your clients' office. Keep this space clean, tidy and uncluttered. From time to time, wipe down your desk to remove crumbs or coffee stains. Try to purchase cable management clips and letter holders to keep the clutter down and give yourself some extra space.

This space is being offered to you temporarily, but that does not mean you cannot make it your own or add items that may assist your productivity like a mini white board or a few extra device chargers. Do not hesitate to provide your own ergonomic keyboards and mouse if those are tools that allow you to work more comfortably. If the space is shared by others or when it comes time to wrap up the project, just be sure that you leave everything as clean and tidy as you found it.

Coffee

Learn to use the coffee machine effectively if you plan to drink coffee in the office. There will be many long hours and sleepy mornings where you will require a cup of Joe just to function. There will also be many small catch ups and meetings that take place over coffee as well. Proper office etiquette is to replace and refill the pot if you are the last one to take a cup and finish the pot. Instructions may vary from machine to machine but the basics remain the same. Hot Water + Coffee Grinds = Drinkable Coffee.

1. Check the water reservoir, if there is one, to be sure there is water in the machine.
2. Add a paper filter to the coffee filter section. You may need to slide or pop this section out of the machine to find it.

3. Add the appropriate amount of coffee grind into the filter. You want to measure about 2 tablespoons of coffee for every 6 ounces of water, which is just shy of one cup.
4. Press 'Brew'. Make sure the pot or container is empty and washed out before reusing. You don't want overflow or mixing with old cold coffee that may have been sitting out over the weekend.
5. Enjoy!

Coffee Disasters

Transitioning to the workforce after nearly two decades in school had me quick to pick up the habit of needing a cup of coffee in the morning to get going. I had never needed to make my own cup in the past and the first few months at the new client always presented a full or semi-full pot of coffee for me to enjoy.

Then, one morning, I showed up and the opaque pot appeared empty. I looked at the machine and debated waiting until someone made a new pot or if I could manage to sort out how the machine worked and do my part and complete the task myself. I had seen some folks operate the machine a few times and I had earned two degrees in college, so I told myself I should be able to figure this one out myself. I added some coffee to the filter, refilled the water, closed the lid and hit 'brew'. Simple enough. I was pretty proud of myself once the machine started to brew. About 75 percent of the way through, the pot began to overflow and the machine just kept pumping out coffee. In a panic, I grabbed my cup and intercepted the flow. As soon as the cup filled up, I spun around and poured it into the sink. By the time I made it back to the machine, the pot was overflowing onto the counter again. I grabbed a second cup and began an "I Love Lucy Routine" of pouring and dumping into the sink. In my panic, I quickly realized the pot had not been completely empty and I had not dumped the leftovers out, causing the pot to now overflow. In a last-ditch effort, I pulled the power plug for the machine from the wall but not before I had made a significant mess in the room. Clearly embarrassed, I cleaned up a bit and back stepped out of the room hoping no one witnessed the 8 AM breakroom chaos with a valuable office etiquette lesson learned.

The Microwave and Fridge

Every corporate office will have a break room. In that break room you will find a water cooler, a coffee machine and a refrigerator at a minimum. Those are there for you to use without asking permission. But as the consultant and not the employee, you will want to be sure you treat these facilities with the same respect you would your own. Wipe down the microwave after every use. Do not keep old food in the fridge overnight and wipe down counters if you make a mess.

TRAVEL

90% Travel Required

One of the best parts of a young consulting career, especially early on, is the ability to hop on a plane to some cool new destination Monday to Thursday, live in a hotel, eat foods you could never afford in college and get to work in cool new places every few months or years. It is fun and exciting and the days do go by a lot faster. Most traveling projects will require you to wake up on Monday at 4:30 AM to catch the 6:00 AM flight to your destination so you can get in as much billable time as possible. On the other side of the week, you will probably be catching the Thursday evening flight out to maximize your day as well. Most projects do not require you to stay until Friday, but from time to time it may be expected. Fair warning, however, the travel can be mentally and physically exhausting at times and definitely does become harder to do as you get older and settle down in life.

Paying the Bills

While you travel, you will be expensing all costs you incur to the client. This is usually done at the end of the month when your firm invoices the client for billable time and expenses. The cadence can vary based on accounting and other agreements. Some firms will issue you a corporate credit card you can use for travel so you are not having to put up the cash yourself.

These costs should rarely be out of pocket. It is very difficult for someone to put up thousands of dollars a month to pay for travel and expenses outside of the home office of employment. In the odd case they are not immediately reimbursed, remember to keep a record of everything that you paid for as a business expense so that you will be able to claim those on your taxes at the end of the year. In general, if you are not able to float the travel cost and you are asked to do so without being given a corporate credit card, make your concern known early and see if you can have a manager or executive assistant help book your travel.

Expense Reports

At the end of each month, you will be required to fill out an expense report. This activity will be one of the more mundane and tedious job requirements you will have but you will want to be reimbursed for the large sums of money you put up for weeks of airfare, food and hotels. Make it a habit to keep receipts as you go. It helps to have a dedicated credit card for work travel so transactions may electronically get recorded in one place. Depending on how strict your auditing department is, you may also need to provide scans of physical receipts as well. There are many apps available to help make this easier or you can just take pictures on your phone as they come in and sort it out later. Most major hotels and airlines will email you a copy of your receipt so you should be able to dig those out of your email when you need the documentation. On the reports themselves, you will need to record the expense, the date, the service, the cost and possibly provide details in the notes.

Once submitted, there is usually an approval process by the payroll and invoicing team. Once approved, you will receive the dollar amount on your next paycheck. This amount should be untaxed and not paid as a bonus or your base pay.

Credit Card Perks

If given the option to not use a corporate card, I would recommend getting your own. Credit cards usually give you thirty to sixty days to pay off the balance, so if you keep up with your expense reports, you should be able to keep a zero balance on the card. This will prevent you from racking up interest fees that would come out of your pocket. Go online and shop around for different credit cards. There are hundreds of cards, some that are free, some with different point structures and some that have an annual fee. Do not rule out annual fee cards right off the bat. A lot of these cards come with better perks. Try to use your consulting skills to create a spreadsheet of pros and cons. The goal is to maximize your net gain and there are many ways to gain on credit cards. Just want some extra cash? Get a card with higher cash back rewards. Want to travel for personal reasons and not just work? Get a card that gives 2x or 3x reward points on travel rewards. Be sure to review the entire guide of perks as well per card. Many offer purchase protection on electronics, flights, free concierge and lounge access at airports which is a must-have if you are prone to getting delayed a lot. All these perks can definitely make some of the longer travel days just a little less painful.

Double Hop Travel
If you want to save some cash on your personal travel and have some flexibility, try the weekend getaway trip while on the road. Instead of flying home, you can usually fly somewhere else as long as you fly back to your client on Monday and the cost difference is the same. If there is a cost difference, cover the difference out of pocket and only expense what it would have cost for you to fly home. This is a good way to save on the airfare of personal travel and get some cool experiences in. Remember to pack accordingly as you will not have a chance to go home and do laundry for about 11 days if you do this kind of trip.

Travel Efficiency
Being able to quickly navigate an airport is one of the most critical skills you will need to have in order to be a traveling consultant. There are many unavoidable red tape and security protocols all airports have and they continue to grow more strenuous as time goes on, so you are going to want to take advantage of every tip and trick in the book to be able to get in and out as fast as you can, or you will be spending a lot of your life standing in line behind a family of

four on their way to Florida who keep getting sent back through the metal detector.

1) Never check a bag. Your usual trip should be three nights and four days. There is no reason you should need more than a single carry-on size bag and your laptop bag. Checking a bag creates extra time overhead when getting to the airport and requires you to be there earlier. It means you have to deal with an extra kiosk which is one more additional line you could have avoided. Once you land, you will have to wait for your checked bag to arrive and you have to deal with the risk of the airlines possibly losing your bag. The time loss and risk is not worth checking a bag and should only be done so if you absolutely have to bring an item with you that is not allowed to fly. If you have a special type of shampoo you need, make a trip to your local superstore. You can purchase empty travel size containers for under a dollar which you can then transfer your liquids into prior to your trip. Remember, if you are traveling with a team, you do not want to be the one everyone needs to wait for as you deal with your checked bag.

Other items that you will need to pack will be three days of business clothes (you should be wearing the first day's clothes on the morning you leave). Things may get a bit creased in a small bag but hotels will have an iron waiting for you in your room. If you are rushed for time, giving creased clothes a good steaming in the bathroom shower always works well. You will probably need a few gym clothes and a pair of running shoes if you plan to work out. It helps to keep a few laundry bags as you will not want your stinky workout clothes mingling with your work clothes on the trip back home. I've survived many years of traveling with just these core basics. All my technology and books travel with me in my laptop bag.

2) Pick an airline, stick with it and be loyal to it. Traveling with the same airline will not only earn you points for personal travel, but the higher loyalty status you earn, the easier and more comfortable traveling becomes. You will be allowed to board the plane earlier, pick better seats closer to the front with more leg room, be able to get off the plane sooner and, from time to time, score an upgrade to first-class. In the scenario your flight is cancelled, you usually end up getting bumped up higher in line for the next flight out which helps avoid getting stuck at the airport for hours on end or, even worse, over night!

3) On a similar note, never book the last flight out on a Thursday night unless your client obligations absolutely require you to. In the case that your flight is cancelled, and it will happen from time to

time, it gives you a few more flights later on to get bumped to without getting stuck at the airport overnight.

4) Car loyalty have similar reward perks programs like the airlines. The most convenient of the rental car perk is getting notified directly to your phone as to where your car is waiting for you. Gone are the days of even needing to talk to someone at the counter. Just walk right to your car and head right out. On the way back in, there is no need to wait for a customer service rep to sign you back in. Just be sure to leave the keys in your car and your receipt will show up in your email as soon as they scan it, which usually happens before you reach your gate.

5) Hotel loyalty also comes with a nifty app. You should be able to check in before you walk through the door and have a key card waiting for you. Newer apps on your phone may allow you to open your hotel door, so needing a key card might not be necessary. This is especially helpful on the long travel Mondays when you just want to get to your room and finally relax. Or in my case, change clothes and get a workout in before dinner.

6) Airport pre-check and clearance is worth the cost. This program does come with an initial cost and an interview with security but usually lasts for five years. Ask your employer if this is something you can expense, or check with your credit card as some may allow you to credit the cost as a perk. This clearance allows you to go through security screening through a special fancy line which usually has significantly less people and is usually faster. Once you get to the metal detectors, they will often let you keep your shoes on as well as let you keep your laptop in your bag when it goes through the X-Ray machine, rather than have to take it out in its own bin, wasting time and risking damages.

Ride Sharing

A great way to travel in the modern age is to utilize a ride sharing app. A rental car can run you and your client around eighty dollars a day with taxes and airport fees. For a fraction of the cost you could just call a ride share from your phone to get where you are going. Besides being able to save the time of having to pick up a rental car and drop one off, you can save the time and cost of filling up the tank on return. Adding up the rides you require for lunch, hotel and other outings from the client site, the cost can be nearly half of what it would be to rent a car. If you share the cost with other teammates it can be even cheaper. You will save time and the client will save money. Another win-win.

Dining

Since you will be on the road, you will be dining out. A lot. I've tried to get creative about bringing granola bars and other dry snacks with me on the road but most of the meals you eat will be at franchises and restaurants. The cost you incur by eating out can get high, but since you are traveling for work, all of your meals will be reimbursed. Each city you are staying in will have a different rate per diem (latin for "per day") for how much you can spend on food daily. Although it may feel nice to burn through that entire dollar amount, you do not necessarily need to if you are concerned about your health or waistline. Some clients will consider your per diem as a "use it or lose it" policy so if you were given sixty dollars a day, and you only used forty dollars that day on meals, then that was the end of that. Other clients will consider the per diem as the default amount you get that day. So, if you were given sixty dollars a day, and you only used forty dollars that day on meals, you can still expense the full sixty dollars and earn an extra twenty dollars untaxed for every day you were on the road. Be sure to verify with your project director before you complete your expense report for the month on what the policy in place is.

Eating out at restaurants usually comes with larger food portions than what is considered a normal healthy portion. Try to cut your meal in half if you can. It may seem wasteful since most hotels will not have a fridge to take the second half home. Even if it does, it can be difficult to take leftovers to a client on the road that may not have a microwave.

When you dine with clients, be sure you always pick up the tab. Even though you may be charging the amount right back to them in the end, it is still one of the major rules of consulting that a client should never pay for a meal. Try not to order the most expensive steak on the menu either, even if you see the client splurging a bit. Even though he may recognize the cost is not coming out of his pocket, it is coming from the company he represents and seeing you act carelessly outside the client office will reflect on your perception at the client office.

If you are out to dinner with your team and the client is not around, feel free to kick back a little. Traveling is hard and can be stressful. Dinner after long hours is a good time to relax and take a break from the work. It's not unusual to head back to the hotel after dinner and do some more work, so give yourself the hour at dinner to watch the game or catch up with your coworkers socially, you deserve it.

Staying in Shape

We previously discussed how to make sure you have your basic essentials with you for working out while on the road. Working out on a Monday after waking up at 4:30 AM, travelling and working a full day does require a lot of willpower, discipline and maybe some coffee. I am hoping I do not have to lecture you on the benefits of working out, but making sure you stay in shape while on the road should be a high priority for you. It is not hard to get carried away with the expensed food and meals, and giving in to the extra fatigue of being on the road. It does not take long to put on the consultant 15 or 20 depending on how poorly you eat.

Most hotels will have some kind of gym. They are usually about 600 square feet and are nothing to brag about, but it should, at the bare minimum, contain a treadmill, an elliptical, a few weights and an area to do floor exercises.

If weather and location permit it, try going for a run outside. It's a great way to see new places and cities. Staying in shape and working out is also a good way to clear your head before or after work. You will feel better overall in work and play.

Being Kind while Traveling

Please remember to be kind when travelling. Travelling will lose its charm at some point and long flight delays, odd eating pattern and lack of sleep will take its toll on you. You will be tempted to chew out the flight agent for not getting upgraded or the hotel service for taking too long to deliver your room service. Try to remember these items are out of the control of the staff member you are planning on berating. Everyone is just doing their job, and no one is going out of their way to specifically screw you over. The flight that is delayed for you is delayed for one hundred and fifty other people and yelling or cursing is not going to get the flight out of maintenance earlier. You accepted a job in consulting with travel expected and these delays will come with the territory, so please try to exercise some patience when things do not go perfectly.

A Little Kindness goes Along Way

Another classic consulting Thursday evening at the airport. A flight is delayed...flight delayed some more...flight finally cancelled. Passengers groaned as the flight cancellation was announced and began to line up at the customer service desk to determine their options on getting home. A large man who was visibly upset pushed his way through to the front of the line where he demanded a seat on the next flight out. The agent politely told him there was nothing she could do and the system would auto assign passengers based on availability. He continued to fume and mentioned his travel status with the airline while screaming at the poor agent. After a few minutes he finally gave in and stomped away, while still yelling curses at the agent, the airline and anyone in his way.

The gentlemen next inline walked up to the deflated agent and said "I guess there is no space on the next flight huh? It is, what it is. Sorry about that other guy".

She looked up and replied, "one minute".

After a few moments of typing away on her computer she handed the gentleman a new boarding pass for the next flight out with a smile. It was the first I had seen anything like this occur but it really showed me in life that there are moments where "you catch more flies with honey".

PEOPLE AND PERSONALITIES

This section will cover some of the high-level personalities you will find throughout your career. These are not meant as a stereotype and every person is different in some form or fashion, but the overall personality types should prepare you for what to expect at your clients' site.

Personalities

The Go-Getter

The Go-Getter is the A-type personality who is an always-working, never-sleeping overachiever. This person is usually hardwired to push themselves and others around them to succeed. It can be in your favor to align yourself with people like this in the organization and cherry-pick some of their traits that will allow you to succeed. They will be great allies to have around and can have road blocks cleared in your work, hammer out items that are perceived to be difficult and keep the project and work moving forward. They have a hard time letting tasks stall out. Be careful, however, as A-types can be perceived to have a lack of empathy. They may push you and others around them a little too hard and cause some friction. Their goal of ultimate success may also lead them to push everyone out of their way and play a bit more of a political or cut-throat game in the work environment.

The Grouchy IT Guy

The grouchy IT guys exist in almost every organization. He usually lives in the IT organization, wears ironic pop culture t-shirts and seems to always be upset about something. Other departments are not safe either as there are equivalent counterparts everywhere in the organization. There is not much you can do when dealing with the grouchy IT guy. He is surly, loves to complain about everything wrong in the organization and usually enjoys crushing diet cokes all day. It will play in your favor to stay as much on their good side as possible, especially if they will play some role on your project, whether it is technical advisory or conducting code deployments. Do not let it get you down when you feel like you are not liked or appreciated by this person. Don't worry, he does not like or appreciate anyone. If his attitude does actually become a hindrance on your work or creates a hostile environment which you are uncomfortable with, raise the concern with your project leadership and see if they are willing to talk to the client sponsor to help resolve the issue.

Remember, everyone goes through some sort of personal life problem from time to time, so don't let it get under your skin and be patient where you can.

The Person that should Avoid Buses

Every company and client is going to have one or a few folks who others will tell you "we don't know what we will do if he/she gets hit by a bus". This person has a vast and profound knowledge of the business and is known as the subject matter expert. There is no type of documentation you can read to get the amount of comprehension this person has in their head. They are absolutely vital to the projects' successes and usually will be happy to share their wisdom with you, if they feel like it will help them grow the organization they have invested so much in. Many times, they are just looking to help you offload some of the dependency on themselves which can be stressful for them.

You may also find the opposite attitude where the subject matter expert is standoffish, and feel threatened by the consultant as the work you are doing may appear to reduce the dependency their employer has on them and fear it may make them expendable. It is best to work in a partnership with folks like these and earn their trust over time. There usually is never enough project work to ever really replace people like these in the organization. Just make sure they avoid the 305 local bus if it doesn't stop in time.

Chatty Kathy
Chatty Kathy takes water cooler talk to the extreme and then will continue to talk until the sun goes down. The topics will range from work related to weekend plans or to the life happenings of her cats. I am clearly stereotyping Kathy here, but this personality is found in men and women alike and the topics of discussion can vary from day to day or person to person. They usually have a hard time knowing when to end conversations and taking nonverbal cues for

when the other person may be trying to exit the conversation. You may not even get in a single word or care to want to get a word in, but this person can often carry on a conversation with themselves for a very long time. Out of politeness, many of us will smile, nod and listen rather than end the conversation. This is all client time that is being wasted that could be used on more important things. As mentioned before, having some form of comradery with others is essential to your success, but spending hours a week having your ear talked off is not a good use of billable time. If you have a hard time ending these conversations, it is perfectly ok to kindly mention you have something you need to get back to at your desk. If you are cornered at your desk, a simple white lie of needing to prepare for an upcoming meeting or a restroom break, or a trip to the kitchen for some water can usually force the break in conversation that you may need to escape. Beware, if you end up with a stage five clinger, as they may even follow you to the restroom or kitchen. At this point, you will need to dance the fine line of being stern on ending the conversation but be sure to let them down easily.

Grinders

The term 'grinders' is used synonymously with the client from hell. They usually work their consultants really hard and for long hours. They are never appreciative and may even speak harshly and negatively to the team, no matter how good of a job they do. Nothing is ever good enough. Do not let grinders get you down or discouraged. In your career, you will have many engagements with a client on some level of the grinder spectrum and they cannot be avoided. Do your best and accept that you may be in an unwinnable situation and you should not be held accountable by your firm or your project manager. If you feel like the folks on your management team are unaware of the situation, do not hold your tongue. Send an email of your concerns early on and see if they can assist in easing the pain. If not, you will have documented evidence of acknowledging the situation and will not be held accountable if things do go south. Remember, not all projects last forever and for years on end. Hopefully, once you roll off the client from hell, the next project will be a lot better!

Unsure New Guy

Unsure new guy or gal never feels confident or sure of what they are doing. They will email you before making any decision, or walk over and ask you if it is acceptable to send you an email about being unsure about making a decision. You will be conflicted in wanting to be a helpful coach, mentor or subject matter expert, but the constant interruptions will take a toll on your focus and productivity. In the beginning it is best to show some patience. Give the support he or she needs and answer the questions they may have. Remember, at some point you were probably the one asking the questions and without others proving you answers and guidance, you would not be where you are. Try to set up touch points or meeting and bundle all their questions into those blocks of time to avoid the constant pings. If overtime, they do not get their feet under them and become self-supported or confident enough to take initiative, it may require some more hands on mentorship from leadership to get things going. There will be a point where you become more of a baby sitter then a mentor and at that point it would be best to have some harder conversations with the resource that maybe consulting may not be the right fit for them.

People and Roles

Business Analyst

As a new consultant, your role will mirror most closely to that of the business analyst. The business analyst will play a large variety of roles on the project and really is considered the Jack of all trades. Their job is to understand and analyze the different functions of the business. They will be responsible for conducting all meetings and interviews to understand and document the knowledge of the business processes and their intersection with strategy and technology. It is not rare to find the business analyst facilitating the project manager with his day to day tasks, or assisting with basic technical development, testing and training. Be prepared to flex your muscles in versatility.

Technical Analyst

The technical analyst's role is a lot more focused on the technology side than his or her business counterpart, although there is a large overlap between the two roles. The technical analyst is responsible for helping to document technical requirements, designing and developing systems and seeing them through to deployment and support. Team members in this role usually have some form of background in development languages or design, but do not let that shy you away from the role if you have not had any experience in the past. From an entry-level, there are many paths that will allow you to move into the technical analyst role over time if this is of interest to you.

Quality Assurance

The quality assurance team is responsible for testing all deliverables and putting all requirements through the ringer to be sure that the end product is working as originally designed and intended. During the requirements phase, the QA team will usually design and create test scripts which meticulously outline the scenarios and steps required for each requirement to be considered a pass or fail.

The actual testing of the requirements, with the help of the quality assurance team, usually occurs during the project phase called UAT or User Acceptance Testing. In this phase, the users work with quality assurance and go through the test scripts previously created. If all scenarios come to a pass, the phase is considered complete and usually kicks off the move of all code and deliverables to production.

Sales

The sales team member's primary role is to keep the work funnel full. They are responsible for finding new projects and prospective clients.

Good salespeople will engage their consultants, business and technical analyst to help them sell projects. Being able to speak to the potential client's business analyst, technical resources, managers and executives will require credibility and they will appreciate the help from non-salespeople to come in and talk the talk. Forging good relationships with the sales team is always valuable as they can help open up doors and progress you through your career outside of client work. A very visible KPI that you will be measured against as you move higher in your firm will be how much work you sold and how much revenue you have generated. Getting this experience in early, even before you are measured against it, will be a valuable lesson.

The Partner

The partner at your firm is usually the highest-ranking role one can achieve. Once someone receives partnership, they usually become a co-owner at the firm. Depending on the size and the partnership program, this can be a very small or a very large percent of ownership stake. This allows the partner to share in company profits and are incentivized to help the company grow. From time to time, the partner will make an appearance at your client's office to shake hands and meet the team. Their role at this level is dependent on making and keeping relationships. The more work they can sell and oversee, the better the firm does, which is better for everyone in the firm's food chain. As a younger consultant, do not be scared or shy to forge a relationship with a partner. They are great allies to have and can help you grow in your career. They can provide guidance and get you promoted. They are always looking for great consultants to staff when they sell a new project as their reputation and salary may be on the line. You will want to be on their short list of people that are cherry-picked when they sell a new project. Only a very few consultants will survive the years and work at a single firm to become a partner. It can be easier to achieve by gathering experience at multiple firms and climbing the consulting ladder over many hard-working years.

Project Manager

The project manager's role on the project is written in his/her title. They oversee the execution of a project and making sure the project is successful. Their role is to manage the day to day tasks and ensure the project is completed on time and on budget. They will often start the day making sure the team is working on the right items and facilitating meetings that may need to take place. They will track weekly burn rate and spend vs. the agreed upon time and budget. When tasks or requirements change (and they will), the project manager is also responsible for helping the client set new priorities, timelines and expectations. Usually, there is no such thing as over-communicating or documenting when playing the project manager role.

A good project manager is also responsible for the health and happiness of the project teams. They will shield you from client scope changes, interruptions and make sure you have a clear path in front of you to do the work.

If the role of project manager is something that interests you, see if you can help them with some of their day to day tasks which they should be happy to share. It will alleviate some of their work as well as give you valuable experience that you will be able to use later on.

Project Sponsor/Stakeholders

The project sponsor is the representative on the client side who owns the project, deliverable or initiative. They are the ones justifying the cost to the business against the value of the project. They are the ones that pushed the project through budgeting and got it signed and started. Their butts are on the line to be sure the project is completed.

The project sponsor may not be involved in the day to day tasks of the project, but as a consultant on a project, you will be required to provide periodic updates and status reports to the sponsor on progress, budget, changes and anything of importance worth mentioning. Usually, your project manager will be responsible for presenting this content, but it is not unusual to find your director or even the partner representing your firm to attend these meetings.

BUSINESS SKILLS

This section covers the basics of major business units and functions at a very high level. It is encouraged that you go off on your own and conduct in-depth research or purchase some basic collegiate level books to brush up. The better-rounded you are across many different business functions, the more valuable you will be to your clients and firm.

Accounting

At the center of every business, you will find the accounting team. Every businesses' core goal is to generate revenue and although they may not want to, spend some money as well. The accounting team's core responsibility is to record and maintain all transactions that occur and keep all financial records. Their processes are daily, monthly, quarterly and yearly. They are the ones making sure that the money flowing in and money flowing out is being tracked, tagged and recorded correctly and that everything ticks and ties. Below are some basic terms and processes you should be familiar with. This by no means is a comprehensive list. A good accounting 101 book from a used bookstore should be common reading when starting your consulting career.

1) GAAP – GAAP stands for generally accepted accounting principles. These rules and processes are common principles, standards and procedures that companies follow when creating their financial statements. For the most part, they are standard

and align across all companies and businesses that follow GAAP.
2) Journal Entry – All financial transactions are recorded in what is called the journal. This is the listing of all financial transactions, where they occurred, the amount they occurred for, and the date they occurred. Journal entries, once entered, should not be removed or deleted as a best practice. To correct an error, a negative entry or adjustment is made so the summation ties out at month-end.
3) General Ledger – The general ledger is the primary record of all accounting transactions for the company.
4) Month-end – The month-end (or quarter/year-end) is the process of finalizing and booking all journal entries, transactions and financial statements at the end of the period. The financial statements must only contain the revenue and expense for the current month. This is also referred to as Monthly Close and it does not always occur on the first day of a new month. Many times, due to inefficient processes or dependencies, month close can occur 15, 30 or more days out.
5) Accounts Receivable – All money that is owed to the company
6) Account Payable – All money that is owed by the company

Operations and Supply Chain

The operations team is a fairly vague term and the roles and responsibilities of the team varies from company to company. The operations team's function can be best described as doing all things related to actually running the business. It can range from packing boxes, buying and selling, dealing with customers or employees and making sure all the gears are turning quickly and efficiently. Consulting projects that work with operations are usually in the space of organizational efficiency and strategy. It will be your job to inject yourself into an operational process and help them eliminate redundancies, inefficiencies and help tasks get done with less manpower and hours. This is where you get to be very creative and help fill holes that others may not have seen. There will be people who have been doing their job the same way for years just because "it has always been done that way", and it is up to you to help suggest and implement a better way of doing the job.

Information Technology (IT)

The IT team is the term used to cover all things technology and data at the organization. They will be responsible for all technical systems in place to run the operational processes, whether the technology is owned and hosted onsite or even if the technology is contracted out via a 3rd party. The IT team will be on the hook for making sure things stay online, run smoothly and continue to add and grow to meet the needs of the business and its respective business units. Automation of people and processes is a big driver and goal for having a well-structured IT department. For all menial tasks you can free up via IT, you will allow employees to better spend their time growing the business in other ways. Under the umbrella of IT, you will also find the data teams. These teams are responsible for managing all the data going in and out of the technology systems. The data teams will provide analytics and insights on how the company is performing and make suggestions on how the systems can possibly perform better. Innovation in IT is what creates the justified spending in consulting projects. Being able to bring in experts and non-full-time employees to build, stand up and support new applications and processes in IT is usually some of the best fits for consulting relationships.

Human Resources

The human resources departments of an organization are responsible for the management of hiring and maintaining all staff. Once an employee is hired, the HR team will support the employee through their entire lifecycle while they are employed. In the beginning, they will help with the onboarding of new employees, training and making sure all initial processes and forms are inline so workers can begin their new careers. Once the initial set up is complete, the HR team will also be responsible for administering payroll and benefits. From the day to day, they will help remediate issues, deal with operational support, manage complaints and ethical violations, help keep the peace and make sure people stay happy and productive. On the back end of the employee's life cycle, they can help with transitioning people out—which is a nice way of saying firing people— or dealing with employees who quit.

As a consultant dealing with HR, many projects will revolve around operational efficiency in HR as well as providing a hiring and firing strategy that aligns with the growth goals set by your project. This team is probably the most connected to the feelings and emotions of others so it will take a certain balance between professionalism and empathy to deal with these kinds of projects.

Management

The management team spans many and all levels of the organization. If someone has a job to do, there will be someone needed to manage them. Even managers have managers and at the top of the managerial food chain sits the C-Level suite. The overall goal of a successful manager is to make sure his or her team is performing their jobs to the best of their ability and that they are happy and the goals of the team align with the overall goal of the organization.

Consulting projects that align with the managerial or C-level suite typically revolve around efficiency and strategy. Consultants will be involved in making sure goals are set correctly and realistically at the top level. They will be responsible for creating and implementing the execution of all agreed upon strategies and changes. These types of projects usually tie to bottom line revenue and profit and loss will be highly visible and an expected goal. You will usually find many senior members of your firm supporting you on these types of projects, especially if you are dealing with the executives of a company.

BUSINESS SKILLS THROUGH THE LIFE OF A PROJECT

The life of a project can span from two weeks to two years. You may be involved in a few of phases and then rolled off to another project or you may be lucky enough to see a project from inception through to completion. No matter what the scope, there are always a few core phases that a project will go through which are outlined below.

Roadmap

Before a project can begin, it must be envisioned. This may sound like hippie mumbo jumbo, but the phase 0.1 of a project is called the roadmap phase. This usually ranges from two to six weeks where the strategy and business analyst team spends their time on as many fact-finding interviews from the top of the organization to the bottom in order to help unearth as many issues, problems and inefficiencies they can discover. They will also discover and document what the current and future goals of the organization are. With these two pieces of information, the deliverable of the roadmap phase will be prepared. It will outline all initiatives and projects that must take place (and in what order) so that the organization can track toward the goals it is setting for itself and eliminate as many of the hurdles that may stand in their way. A good roadmap will be very detailed, include high-level time-frames, a high-level budget, and demonstrate how the projects will be structured. In a small sense, this is the sales cycle 2.0. Many projects never make it past the roadmap phase due to reasons such as sticker shock on the price, lack of buy-in on the long-term vision from the leadership or just a misalignment of what the company goals are or what the real problems are. If successful, the roadmap will foray very nicely into the requirement gathering phase.

Requirements and Requirement Gathering

The first phase of a project will revolve around requirement gathering. During this time, you will meet with users, team members, managers and project stakeholders to ask questions and begin to document people and processes to create an outline of what it is you will be creating or designing. Requirement documents will then be used to shape the project deliverables, create timelines and help create a clear understanding between you and the client and the goals for the project. It is usually advised that all requirements are signed off by the stakeholders before proceeding to the next steps to prevent anyone marching in the wrong direction. As the project progresses, these requirement documents will pass from the business analyst to the technical team, functional team, testers and end users, creating a single point of truth and continuity for the project goals. The best requirements will typically be written at the task level and have sub-requirements written at more atomic levels if the task allows itself to be broken down. This will permit work to be split across resources more effectively and allow for more clarity during the testing phase.

A Functional requirement will outline what the system or process is supposed to actually do. It will outline what the system must do, how it must behave, how it is expected to react to failure and how it provides the business value.

A Technical requirement will be based on all the technical functions that the system must perform or fulfill. It will outline all coding standards, logical operations, technical specifications and dependencies on development order or impacts to other systems and processes.

A good requirement document will have the following sections:

1) The Author, Created Date, Date Last Modified and some form of Revision Log.
2) Overview and Scope
    a. What is the objective of the requirement and what does it cover? It will need to answer the questions of what the requirement is, who it is for and why it is needed.
3) Assumptions and Risk
    a. Not all questions will have answers when a requirement is written and you may never be able to document all the gaps and holes you are trying to fill. In this section, be sure to list out all items you are making an

assumption on, and carefully walk the client through those assumptions. If something is incorrect, the client will either surface the answer for you or will sign off on the assumption and the risk it creates. This way, if something goes awry later on down the road due to something or some system behaving not as you originally expected, it will justify a change order or a change in direction without scrutiny from the client.
4) Dependencies
    a. This section will list out all other tasks, processes and items that must be in place for this requirement to be completed. This will help the project management team prioritize and outline a timeline of requirements that need to be delivered.
5) The Actual Requirements
    a. The actual requirement section can be a simple paragraph or multiple pages with text, diagrams, flow charts and other visual aides to get the message across. There is no wrong answer to how much detail is needed and it is definitely better to lean on the side of caution and over-explain so there is little room for misinterpretation when the requirement is passed on to other team members.
6) Pass Fail Conditions

      a. The passing conditions will relate directly to the signed off requirements. Anything outside of the passing requirements will be considered a fail, so there's no need to explicitly list out every failure scenario under the sun. This section will be the first pass at what will eventually become the test scripts.
7) Glossary
      a. Your requirement document is going to contain a lot of language that is very specific to the client. Each client will use their own acronyms, have their own code names for specific reports or processes and new systems may use all sorts of foreign naming conventions. As you learn about these and put them into your requirements document, do the next guys a favor and keep a good glossary section.

Development and Delivery Phase

Once requirements are wrapped up and signed off, it is time to roll up your sleeves and get to work. During this phase, systems will be designed, codes will be written, processes will be implemented, coffee will be drunk, people will be shuffled around, new roles will emerge and the business will begin to shift in the new desired direction. There will be many late hours and many white board sessions that paint entire walls in dry erase art. The project managers will track the time and hours spent and make sure the ship is headed in the right direction and on the correct schedule, while the business analysts will continue to document findings and adjust requirements. There are a million micro-tasks that take place during the delivery phase and they will vary based on the type of projects. Be sure to use some of the tips and tricks in the following section to help facilitate a successful delivery phase.

Agile Development vs. Waterfall

Project delivery usually follows two different types of methodologies. The first is Waterfall, where the tasks are lined up in succession and in order. The series of tasks are lined up to requirements and core functionality releases. This ends up with longer phases of work but bigger releases to the users. The second method is called Agile, where delivery is completed in sprints usually ranging from one week to three weeks. This methodology lends itself to a more iterative approach with frequent but smaller releases to the users. Both methodologies can be successful and a good consultant will be familiar with both and, more importantly, how to create a hybrid and flexible approach to meet different client cultures, styles and projects. Most projects will lean towards the agile method or some form of very short burst waterfall or phase. It is never a good idea to big bang large waterfall projects that run from six months to one year. This is usually referred to as boiling the ocean and can introduce risk such as the stakeholders losing interest in a project, or getting concerned when they do not receive more immediate benefits of the project they are spending their money on. Also, the more items going live at once means the more spinning plates you will need to keep an eye on and the more things that can go wrong.

Environments, Unit Testing and Releasing to Test

This section applies more to technical and functional projects. Work usually takes place in four major environments: local, development, test and production. The local environment is all the work that happens on your laptop. It is isolated to the processors and hard drive you are working on. You won't have any fears of screwing anything else up for anyone since you are local, but the code and data you are working with will grow stale and make it harder to have a clearer picture of what you are trying to align your work to when you are testing. Local environments are not always necessary if there is a good development environment. This environment is usually shared amongst other consultants and developers, so you may run the risk of stepping on each other's toes even if you have a solid source control strategy in place. This environment is a safe sandbox for you to create new objects or alter existing ones. Business users will never be working with anything in this environment and it will be the most unstable due to the untested elements being worked on or developed.

As you create and develop your items in the development environment, the first phase of testing will take place. This is called unit testing and is done by the consultant or developers. Here is where you hand test the functionality against the definitions outlined in the requirements. You may not have the best data or stable code to work with, but you will be in charge of the first smoke test to be sure things are working the way you designed them to.

Once unit testing is completed, code is then moved to the test environment. Code should be deployed or transitioned to the test environment exactly how it would be to the production environment later on. Testing the deployment process is just one more test you will need to perform in addition to the functionally of the code going over. The test environment should be as close of a mirror to production as possible. The size, speed, tools and data must be copied over or replicated after every major release to be sure your dress rehearsal is as close as possible to the main show. If all goes well during the testing phase, your code will be ready for go live! The production environment will be the actual systems the business users will use day to day and is considered an active part of operations.

In larger organizations and projects, you may have multiple versions of development and test environments for redundancy, scale or just so that you can separate different teams and functions. Be sure to keep a cheat sheet of what goes where as you do not want to be moving code and component over to the wrong area accidentally!

QA and Testing
The quality assurance team will be in charge of testing all new items against the items described in the requirements and then stepping through the test scripts. They will attempt their best to break the product and deviate from any steps to see if the correct error handling is in place. Be warned, the QA team will drive you crazy during this phase. There is also a good chance that you will be the QA team for one of your projects, so please try to be sympathetic towards their obsessive attention to detail as you may be in the same spot later on and it will serve you to be just as meticulous. There is no such thing as overkill in testing as all items caught and remedied here will only lend itself to a more bulletproof end product.

User Acceptance Testing
The User Acceptance Testing phase, commonly abbreviated to UAT, is where the actual users of the system begin to test and validate the systems and processes in place. They will be responsible for ensuring everything has been implemented to the agreed upon requirements. They will click through screens, run reports, compare spreadsheets and ensure all numbers and data ticks and ties to the smallest decimal point. These steps should be outlined clearly in the test scripts and all issues and errors that surface must be submitted back to the QA, development and delivery team. It is not unusual to be in quick fix mode during UAT and this can be the most stressful point of a project as you move towards the finish line. For technical

systems, The UAT testing will occur in the test environment with data and systems copied identically from production. This will allow the users to work with data they are familiar with that has already been validated so that they can compare apples to apples. When the process is brand new, how you determine what qualifies as a "pass" scenario will be defined in the requirements.

Go Live and Deployment

Go live (also referred to as cut over or deployment) is the big show. This is where all the hard work of the project or phase is moved over into the production environment and when processes are implemented in the day to day for release. Go lives will be met with a very detailed and scripted deployment plan that will manage all people, processes and systems. There will be checkpoints and sign-offs as steps go live one after the other. The go live will function similarly to a NASA space shuttle launch. Different items will be greenlighted, kicking off the next set of dependencies until all boxes are checked and it is time for blast off. Even in non-technical projects, without an actual deployment, having people cut over to new ways of doing business must be met with similar diligence.

A good go live will always have a backup and contingency plan. Things can and will go wrong. Things that were missed in testing or new unexpected problems will arise. Go lives are usually met with the entire team standing on guard, watching, participating and testing diligently. There will be lots of hand-holding with the client to get them up and running. No matter how much documentation you have provided, an in-person helping hand will go a lot further. Be prepared to spend some late hours and travel some extra miles. Your reputation is very exposed at this time and the more seamless the transition to production, the better you will look for it.

Support, Documentation and Training

In addition to the requirement and testing documents that have been created, as a consultant, you will also be responsible for creating hand-off documentation as projects and phases complete. These documents will include how-to guides, user manuals, quick reference guides, support strategies and general training material. The actual training artifacts you are on the hook for delivering in regards to documentation will be outlined in the original SOW. It is good to keep blank templates with you in your tool belt as you go from project to project as it will allow you to spin these documents up faster and provide a good list of must-have items to document for every type of project.

You may also be responsible for the actual training portion of the project. For larger, more structured projects, there will be a dedicated training and change management team whose responsibility will be to create all material and ensure that all the new shiny items you have worked so hard to stand up get adopted and used correctly. Many times, projects will fall apart post-deployment if there is a failure in adoption. If the processes and tools seem too difficult for the client due to not having the correct training and understanding, they will quickly complain to their leadership and revert to their old ways of doing their job since that is familiar and seem easier. Helping ease the pain of change is a very critical role for projects and it is not to be undervalued to keep the project from falling apart in the final mile.

DISASTER RECOVERY

A good technology project will need to include a disaster recovery plan. This is a set of processes, procedures and guidelines to be followed in case a critical failure occurs. Maybe a server crashes, or a hard drive fails. I once was at a client where the data center flooded after heavy rain storms. Disaster recovery can also include how to proceed if a team member or support staff is incapacitated for some reason. A good consultant will plan for all contingencies in their solution proposal and delivery.

TOOLS TIPS AND TRICKS

Let's spend some time covering the tools and skills you should have in your consulting tool belt. These can be technology tools, standards, best practices and tips to help you succeed in your day to day and ensure long-term success.

Spreadsheets

The spreadsheet is going to be the most used piece of software you will need on projects, so it is a no-brainer to be caught up on the basics. Because they are so versatile, spreadsheets will not just be used for recording data, but they will be used as reports, trackers, calculation sheets, documentation, maps and a million other things. Let's take a very high-level look at some of the concepts you should be familiar with:

1) Basic math
    a. Learn to use the sum, average, median and count functions. No explanation needed here.
2) Logical
    a. Logical functions such as If/Or statements will be required to allow you to compare items and create new derived columns. These statements will return as TRUE or FALSE based on your conditions and choose the desired effect or outcome based on the result.
3) Look-Ups

a. A look-up is where you compare the rows and columns in one table against the values of another and produce a result. A look-up will come in handy when trying to pair information from multiple sources and create reference points between them.
4) Pivot Tables
   a. A pivot table is a magical thing. Spreadsheet tools will create them automatically on a range of data and create a mini ad hoc aggregating dataset. You will be able to slice and dice your data on the fly and create custom calculations as well. It is a very powerful analytical tool which is a must-learn for all consultants.
5) Charts and Graphs
   a. The human brain is a lot better at interpreting data and trends visually, which is why we get more from looking at charts and graph data than from a million rows of data. Be sure to learn your spreadsheet tool functions on creating visuals based on your data. Remember, there is a right and wrong way to plot data on a chart, so when creating charts, be sure to provide a visual that clearly explains the story and does not leave room for misinterpretation or misjudgment.

If you really want to go expert mode and impress your peers, try to learn the basics of spreadsheet automation and coding. Most have a built-in coding language or Macros that will allow you to turn spreadsheets into working applications. As a consultant, making the process more autonomous and efficient is your primary focus and you will find there are many tasks people perform on a daily basis that can be wired to a single push of a button.

Presentations

The Slides/Decks/Presentation is the primary method of communication between a consultant and a client in the wild. Presentations are mash-ups of words, pictures, and flowcharts that help messages to be communicated. They are used in early sale cycles to illustrate roadmaps, to show weekly progress, to wrap up a project, and for training, just to a list a few examples:

1) Never use a slide transition animation. This may look cool at first, but it cheapens the presentation. Just stick to default which will switch to the next slide immediately.
2) Never show real data on a presentation. You never know if this material will be shared outside your group and you must always keep client data and confidentiality at the top of your mind when including screenshots. Try to blur out anything that may be sensitive or replace it with mock or test data.
3) Keep a good pace and the right amount of material on a single slide. It is very difficult to keep a crowd's

attention, especially with phones buzzing with emails and folk anxious to get to their next meeting to watch yet another presentation. Be clear and concise with the information you present, only keeping the high-level points on the slide. All elaboration should be done as you present.

4) Always use large, readable fonts. If it is hard to read, it will not be read and just adds clutter. If you do need to document additional detail in your slides, add an appendix to the back and email the presentation to all attendees so that they can look for details at a later time.
5) Lean on chart and visuals where you can. People will digest graphs and flowcharts a lot easier than a series of words.
6) If possible, practice before you present. This will allow you to get used to the flow of the presentation and let you gauge the pace you should be following.
7) Shut off all phone alerts, applications and notifications if you are presenting from your computer. You do not want an embarrassing email or chat message being shown off to the room full of clients. To be extra safe, cut off your Wi-Fi before sharing your presentation on a big screen projector.
8) Get the presentation on your desktop before presenting

Remember, there is a way to overuse the presentation as well. It takes time and effort to create a good one and sometimes the message can be as simple as a summary email or a phone call.

Please ignore that

The release 2.0 presentation was coming along great. We were flying through the slides, questions were being answered and executives were actively engaged and not buried in their phones. As I played the role of the speaker, my phone decided to go off, blasting the auto-tuned hip hop remix of the Leprechaun in Alabama theme song. Yes. That is a real song. Google it.

The 10 infinite seconds of smashing my phone to get it to stop were then followed by 10 more infinite seconds of a very confused room of older executives. "Please ignore that" was all I could muster and just began to plow through the set of next slides. Since that day, I have never deviated from the default ringtones, tried to always make sure my phone was off before a big presentation and left the hip hop remixes to my workouts.

Task Tracking and To Do List

A good consultant will always keep one or many to do lists. They will keep these lists up to date and organized. A good strategy will be to frequently add new items to the bottom and spend some time every day reorganizing and reprioritizing this list. Your project manager will keep a project task list, but what you are required to do will be your own responsibility to manage.

As items are completed, be sure to check them off and clear them out to remove the clutter. Additional clutter is known to increase stress and anxiety and nothing feels better than crossing a bunch of items off in a day and bathing in the feeling of accomplishment. Everyone will have slightly different styles of how they self-manage, and I hope you figured that out before you left college. No matter your style, some form of task tracking is a healthy habit to practice and grow to be good at your job, especially at a time when projects are pulling you in multiple directions.

Screen Shares, Video Shares and Conference Calls

As the age of the internet has grown, the ability of businesses to communicate across cities, countries or continents has grown significantly easier. For many calls and presentations, you will lean on the ability to run a conference call with a screen share with your clients and colleges from the comfort of your own office or home. I have a few basic tips (and some warnings) to share here:

1) Always call in and sign in a few minutes early. When you call in, there is usually an automated welcome message which requires you to enter some kind of Pin or ID. If you're anything like me, you will

probably fat finger the wrong code at least twice before getting through.

2) When you sign in to a screen sharing application, there is sometimes a small download and installation that must take place on your computer. All of these can eat up precious minutes and you do not want to keep others on hold while you are catching up.

3) If you are the host of the call, always call in early. The conference line will usually play some form of waiting music so keep the punishment of others to a minimum for dialing into the call before the first person jumps on. This will also allow you to keep track of attendance as people join so you do not have to run a roll call over the phone.

4) Keep your camera covered with a piece of tape. There is nothing more startling than joining an online conference call and having your face broadcast to the group without knowing it. It's easier to activate the functionality once you are ready for it.

5) Without fail, you will have multiple people trying to talk over one another, followed by awkward silences as folks politely wait for someone else to speak. It is good to have a single primary owner who can control the conversation and flow. Try using the built-in shared chat boxes on the screen share tools. This way, you can stockpile questions as you go and then answer them when there is a correct break in the flow of the presentation.

6) Email out all agendas and attachments prior to the meeting. There will be attendees who may not be by a computer or will want to review the material after the call, so it is best to get that out prior or when you originally schedule the conference call.

Topless Terry

All names have been changed for this story to protect all parties' egos and future employment opportunities. Terry began his day with a run during a balmy Texas summer. It was a work from home day for Terry so he knew he could get a quick workout and shower in before settling down for the workday from his home office. Upon returning home, he removed his shirt to cool down and picked up his phone to notice he had been signed up for a conference call demo which started in less than five minutes! With no time to shower, he sat down, booted up his computer and started the online conference meeting. As participants gathered, meeting control was transferred to Terry to show his screen. Once he accepted and began his demo, someone on the line spoke up "ahem, Terry...Terry". "Yes?" Terry replied

"Your camera is on."

From the perspective of everyone on the conference call, the image of topless Terry was broadcast for all to see. It took a second for Terry to realize what was going on before he slammed his laptop shut. Embarrassed, he apologized profusely. Luckily, everyone was a good sport about it and now Terry is plagued with retellings of this story at every company holiday party, but I believe a valuable lesson was learned here for all.

Flow Charts and Process Flows

The flow chart is a very powerful visual tool to help illustrate processes and system integrations. There are many useful tools out there you can use that will provide you with the few basic shapes and arrows you will need.

1) Break flows into separate atomic flows. Once flow diagram to represent a single process. This creates less cluttered presentations. Use different colors, a master flow or an appendix to link all the sub flows together.
2) Do your best to keep the flow as simple as possible. Avoid intersecting lines as best you can to keep your diagram from looking like a complex spider web.
3) Group and color coordinate items as needed, this will give anyone looking at it a quick way to know what items are tied together.
4) Stick to the same few basic shapes. Most of your flowcharts should not need more than the basic squares, circles, cylinders, triangles, arrows and the tiny human-shaped icon to illustrate a person or group. It is ok to get creative with shapes of computers, octagons, buildings or something to further illustrate your point, but be sure it is clean,

clear and not flashy. You should avoid clip art or any sort of animation for those same reasons.

White Boarding

With all the visual methods of communications covered, you may be wondering if consultants ever speak to one another. Another very common method of meeting and communication is called the white boarding session. If you are unfamiliar with the white board, it is the plastic board in meeting rooms which you can draw and color on with dry erase markers. These boards help people draw, mark up, list, categorize, plan and add flow charts on the fly and can be really helpful in requirement gathering meetings to draw out your notes and assumptions for all to see. This is a great way to avoid miscommunications and misinterpretations. Be sure to erase what you draw on the board as a common courtesy to the next team using the room, as well as being sure to remove any sensitive material that you may not want shared with others. Take a picture on your phone before you erase your hard work and email it to all the participants so that everyone can have a copy of the lessons learned.

I for one have the handwriting skills of a two-year-old, so I stick to shapes and arrows. Some offices have entire walls that are coated in special white board paint that allows you to live out your childhood dreams and draw on the walls, but be careful, I've seen consultants mistake a clean white regular wall as one of these special walls and it is never fun to explain to a client why you ruined the paint.

Programming
Now that the digital age is in full swing, the second most common language you will encounter in the business world besides English is going to be some form of a programming language. If you are a new hire entering the consulting work force from a non-technical educational background such as management or economics, do not let that deter you from taking a beginner programming class or reading a book or two on the subject. A highly valuable language to learn will be SQL (Standard Query Language). SQL can be used to query though databases, combine data sets and create calculations. It can be used to extract data and then dump the results to a spreadsheet to perform additional analysis. Learning a language such as SQL will allow you to break your dependency on technical team members and give you the ability to deep dive and analyze the heart of an organization through its data, thus making you a very powerful business analyst.

Focus
Emails, Instant Messenger, Social Media, Work Message Boards, and responding to taps on your cubicle walls will all be enforced as job requirements for consulting, as well as replying to client emails instantly—no matter what time of

the night they appear in your inbox. Some firms will even compensate your cell phone bill, creating the expectation that you are supposed to be glued to your phone after-hours.

What no one tells you is that this level of distraction and multitasking will actually lead to you doing less work. The amount of time it takes the human brain to switch tasks and get into a good rhythm is shorter than the time the next interruption will hit you. Without learning and enforcing personal habits of focus and being able to disconnect and recharge, you will find yourself working longer, doing less and burning out faster. Try to set aside blocks of time of concentrated work where you do not check your email or your social media feed. You will be surprised that clients do not expect you to respond right away and you will not be fired for taking a few hours to get back to people about non-urgent topics as long as you are doing focused, relevant work instead.

INTERVIEW QUESTIONS

Interview questions can range far and in between a large range based on the person, company, and level you are interviewing for at a consulting firm. First round of interviews are probably one-on-one interviews and it is best to prepare ahead of time. Let us look at some popular questions and strategies on how to best answer them.

Tell us about yourself?

This is the classic and most common opening question in all interviews. First impressions mean a lot in all interviews and consulting is no different. Be ready to answer this question in some form or fashion. Start with a quick mention of your education but no need to get into the details of each of the classes you took. Only mention when you graduated and why this is relevant to your interview. For example, you can say you obtained an MBA last Fall since you wished to grow your career and enter the world of consulting for the interesting and challenging opportunities it provides. Mention your professional work history from your resume and highlight as many relevant bullet points that can relate to consulting. Do not deep dive any, as if the interviewer is interested, they will ask you to explain more later.

Do not spend too much time getting into your hobbies or anything unrelated to the position early on. The first question is to determine if you are the right fit before digging further into the details and whether you play hockey on the weekends is irrelevant.

Why are you interested in consulting?

This question is asked to see if you have really done your homework into how a consulting organization works and operates. It is a good thing you have read this book! You are well on your way. The interviewer wishes to know not only how well you understand consulting, but also how you plan to handle the potential negatives such as long hours, travel, and difficult clients. Try to focus your answer on the learning opportunities that only consulting can provide. Explain your interest in opportunities and ability to learn quickly, take on interesting challenges, or how you wish to become a subject matter expert and a trusted advisor in one area. Try to pepper in past anecdotes of experience you may have had that prove you are being genuine in your answer.

Avoid answers such as "I want to travel or have my food expensed". These are not valid reasons you would want to join a firm and show short-sightedness and immaturity in the toll consulting can take.

Tell me about a time you displayed leadership?

No matter what level you join a consulting firm, leadership is a primary skillset you must have. In consulting you will spend a lot of time working in teams to plan, execute, and implement solutions for clients and those all require some degree of leadership. For this answer, have one prepared that highlights a time you had to step up to be a leader and help solve a real problem from your past experiences.

Outline how the different efforts you made contributed to the overall success of the problem at hand.

Tell me about a difficult problem you occurred in the past and how you overcame it?

This question is like the leadership question and should be answered in a similar format. Instead of a scenario of where you had to be a leader, this one is more open-ended to any problem you may have had such difficult teammates, changing deadlines, etc. Have an answer prepared that starts with the issue that had occurred, your role in identifying it and the steps you took to cause a successful resolution.

Why do you want to work for this firm?

This question is designed to test your knowledge of the consulting industry and your motivation for picking a specific firm. Highlight some of the key reasons for your interest in the specific firm you are interviewing with. Do your research before going into the interview. Figure out what areas this firm focuses on and excels in. Be sure to mention those and how those align with your goals and career aspirations. Mention how not only how the company can help you grow and obtain your goals but also how you can help the company grow and obtain theirs.

What are your strengths and weaknesses?
Another common question across many industries. For this question, have 2-3 of each strength and weakness prepared. For the strengths, it is important to show confidence but not arrogance. The goal is to highlight qualities such as focus, dedication, creativity, and relate to how you apply them to your day to day tasks, especially at work. The interviewer is looking to see if what you bring to the table is going to be a fit for the role they are hiring for. In consulting, strengths such as leadership, work ethic problem solving, hard-working are usually ideal.

The weakness portion of the answer is always a little trickier. You want to appear self-aware of your flaws but not list out items that will eliminate you as a candidate. It is also easy to see through "weakness as strength" answers such as "I work too hard". Try to be honest about your answers and mention shortcomings that are not critical and how you have begun to take steps to grow and evolve.

Logical Thinking Questions
Logical questions are usually theoretical or analysis driving questions. The purpose of these questions is not to see if you get the exact right answer but to evaluate your thought process and methodology of problem-solving. Now is not the time to be quiet. Be sure to talk through your solution and draw out your answer as you process the solution. It ok to backtrack if you have gone down a path that does not make sense. Just be sure to show why you feel you made an error and how to correct it. Visuals will be your friend if you

have access to a whiteboard or notepad. Here are some sample questions to give you an idea of what to expect.

- How many airplanes leave from Boston's Logan Airport on Monday?
- How many quarters can fit in this room?
- How many lightbulbs are there in Manhattan?
- How many passengers fly through LAX in a calendar year?

More Questions

Here is a list of more common questions you may see in an entry-level interview. Be sure to practice with a friend and have answers to many of these ready before you show up to your interview.

- Please describe your most important leadership experience and the impact that you had as a leader.
- Describe a problem that you would like to tackle at why, and how would you pursue it.
- If I were to speak to your colleagues from your most recent internship (or friends in school), what would they say about you? What are the strengths and weaknesses they would share?
- Describe a situation where you failed. What did you learn about yourself and how did you change as a result?
- Why our firm instead of your current firm? What do you know about us compared to your firm?
- Tell me about a project that didn't go well and why and what you would do differently next time?

- How do you quantify a lead?
- Can you describe your brand?
- How have you dealt with low team morale in the past? Provide an example of when you had to give a bad performance review.
- Describe a project which challenged you. Describe a client relationship that was challenging.

Conclusion

Looking back at all my years in the workforce, I feel truly lucky to have spent nearly all of it in consulting. I have learned so much and come so far, but as the nature of consulting goes, there is always much more to learn and explore. With every new project comes new people, places, lessons, experiences and challenges that must be overcome. Some of my successes are credited to my own hard work and work ethic, but a lot has come from having the best mentors a person could ask for. I have had the privilege to work with some of the best in the industry and that is my final piece of advice to you. Seek out those Rockstar mentors. They are the ones that take pride in helping others out and are always there to answer questions and provide direction. If you are lucky, they will stay with you throughout your entire career even as you go work for other companies and take on new roles. Take lessons from the good people you come across as well as the bad. Every experience will help shape you and grow as a successful consultant. To all those that have provided me with some form of guidance and even to those that taught me through the school of hard knocks, thank you.

www.ingramcontent.com/pod-product-compliance
Lightning Source LLC
Chambersburg PA
CBHW031426210526
45464CB00005B/2065